Contents

Preface to the Second Edition xi
Preface to the First Edition xiii
Introduction xv

1. An Introduction to Computing 1
   Why was the Computer Invented? 1
   The Machine 3
   Information in the Computer 5
   Input/Output Devices 6
   Characteristics of Computers 7
   1) Speed 7
   2) Storage 8
   3) Accuracy 8
   4) Versatility 9
   5) Automatic 9
   6) Diligence 9

2. The Basic Anatomy Of The Computer 12
   Basic Structure 12
   A Clerical Exercise 14
   Data Representation Within the Computer 15
   Computer 'Words' 15
   Number Systems 17
   Binary Number System 17
   Binary Counting 17
   The Arithmetic and Logic Unit 19
   Computer Arithmetic 19
   Addition 19
   Complementary Subtraction 20
   Arithmetic Section of the ALU 22
   Logic Gates 22
   Logic Section of the ALU 24

Memory Unit   24
    The Purpose of Addressing   24
    Instructions   25
Control Unit   26
    Registers   27
A Computer Installation   27

3. Man-Machine/Machine-Man Communication   30
Input   30
    Path 1: Punched Cards and Paper Tape   32
        a)   Card Punching and Reading   32
        b)   Paper Tape Punching and Reading   34
    Path 2: Mark and Character Recognition   35
        a)   Mark Sense Reading   35
        b)   Magnetic Ink Character Recognition (MICR) 35
        c)   Optical Character Recognition (OCR)   37
    Path 3: Teletypewriter Terminal   38
Output   39
    Printed Output   40
    Graphical Output   40
    Visual Display Units (VDU)   41
        Graphics VDU   42
    Computer Output Microfilm (COM)   43
    Audio Response Unit   44
Backing Stores   44
    Magnetic Tape   44
    Magnetic Disk   46
    Floppy Disk   47
    Input Direct to Backing Stores   49
        a)   Key-to-Tape   49
        b)   Key-to-Cassette/Cartridge   49
        c)   Key-to-Disk   49

4. Principles Of Flowcharting And Program Development   52
    Example 1:   Sequence   53
    Example 2:   Information to be Retrieved   55
    Example 3:   Counting – Population Survey   56

5. Computer Languages   60
    Machine Codes   61
    Assembly Codes   61
    High-Level Languages   62
        Compilation Process   62
    A Short Program   63
        a) Simple Problem   64

COMPUTERS
AND
COMMONSENSE

c?

COMPUTERS AND COMMONSENSE

Roger Hunt and John Shelley
Imperial College of Science and Technology

SECOND EDITION

Prentice/Hall · PHI · International

Englewood Cliffs, New Jersey   London   New Delhi
Singapore   Sydney   Tokyo   Toronto   Wellington

British Library Cataloguing in Publication Data

Hunt, Roger
    Computers and commonsense. — 2nd ed.
    1. Electronic data processing
    I. Title
    001.6'4   QA76

    ISBN 0-13-165381-4

Library of Congress Cataloguing in Publication Data

Hunt, Roger, 1936 —
    Computers and commonsense.

    Bibliography: p.
    Includes index.
    1. Computers, 2. Electronic data processing.
  I. Shelley, John, joint author.   II. Title.
  QA76.H797 1979 001.6'4   78-11361
  ISBN 0-13-165381-4

To Patricia and Rosalind

ISBN 0-13-165381-4

Prentice-Hall International, Inc., *London*
Prentice-Hall of Australia Pty. Ltd., *Sydney*
Prentice-Hall of Canada, Ltd., *Toronto*
Prentice-Hall of India Private Limited, *New Delhi*
Prentice-Hall of Japan, Inc., *Tokyo*
Prentice-Hall of Southeast Asia Pte., Ltd., *Singapore*
Prentice-Hall, Inc., *Englewood Cliffs, New Jersey*
Whitehall Books Limited, *Wellington, New Zealand*

10 9 8 7 6

Typeset by MHL Typesetting Ltd., Coventry.
Printed and bound in Great Britain by A. Wheaton & Co. Ltd., Exeter

    b) High-Level Version   64
    c) Machine-Level Version   66
Logical/Comparison Operations   68
Development of a Computer Program   70
    1) Algorithm   70
    2) Flowchart   70
    3) Code into a High-Level Language   71
    4) Input Preparation   71
    5) Compilation   71
    6) Corrections   71
    7) Testing Process   71

6. **Introduction To Computer And Operating Systems**   74
   Early Computer Configurations   74
   Peripheral and CPU Speeds   75
   Improved I/O Performance   76
   Batch Processing   76
   Operating Systems   78
   Multi-Programming   79
   Time-Sharing   81
   Real-Time   82
   Computer Networks   83
   Distributed Processing   84
Summary   85

7. **Computer Applications**   86
Scientific Research   86
Business Applications   87
   Payroll and Personnel Records   87
   Stock Control and Sales   88
   Banking   89
   Insurance and Stockbroking   90
   An Aid to Management   90
Industrial Applications   91
   Electricity   92
   Steel   92
   Printing and Paper   92
   Engineering Design   93
Meteorology   94
Space Technology   94
Communications   95
   Air Travel   95
   Transportation   96
   Traffic Control   96

Local Authorities and Public Utilities 97
Telephones 97
Medicine 98
Law and Order 99
Libraries and Museums 99
Education 100

8. Data Processing **102**
Data Processing 102
Source Documents 103
Data Input 103
Data Manipulation 103
Output of Information 104
Data Storage 104
Files and Records 104
File Creation 106
File Access 106
File Manipulation and Maintenance 106
File Generation 106
File Organization 107
Sequential 107
Direct 107

9. An Introduction To Systems Analysis **108**
The Development of Systems Analysis 108
The Analyst's Relationship to the Company ... 110
The Analyst's Relationship to the Computer Department 111
Background Knowledge Required by Analysts .. 111
Initiating a System 112
Assignment Brief 112
Steering Committee 112
Feasibility Study 113
Full System Investigation 113
Design, Implementation and Testing 113

10. The Organization Of A Data Processing Department ... **115**
Design (Systems Analysis) 115
Development (Programming) 116
Operations 116

11. The Social Issues **120**
Information Processing 120
Efficiency/Productivity 120
Automation 122

Privacy/Individuality   123
Security   123
Conclusions/Future   124

APPENDICES

1. **The Development Of Computers**   128
Tabulating Machines   129
The Advent of Digital Computers   129
  HARVARD MARK I   129
  ENIAC   130
  Von Neumann   131
  EDVAC   131
  Manchester Mark I   132
  EDSAC   132
Computer 'Generations'   132
Computer Manufacturers   135
  UNIVAC   135
  IBM   136
  CDC   136
  Burroughs   137
  HIS   137
The Development of the U.K. Industry   137
  ICL   138
Mini-computers   138
Micro-computers   139

2. **Programming Languages**   141
  FORTRAN   141
  ALGOL   143
  Pascal   143
  COBOL   143
  PL/1   144
  RPG   144
  APL   145
  BASIC   145

3. **Decision Tables**   146
Example 1: Servicing a Car   146
Example 2: Mail Ordering   147
Conclusions   150

4. **BASIC**   152
Elements of the BASIC language   152

Summary of BASIC commands   153
Program Examples   154
    Example 1:   Program to find the average of three
                       numbers   155
    Example 2:   Programe to perform search for book
                       title   155
    Example 3:   Program to convert fahrenheit temperature
                       readings to centigrade   158

Glossary   161
List Of Acronyms   163
Bibliography   165
Index   167

Preface
TO THE SECOND EDITION

Computing is not a subject to remain dormant for any length of time and many technological advances have taken place over the three or four years since this book was first published. In order to reflect these changes, the authors, with the kind permission of their publishers, have produced a second edition.

The material has not changed in any fundamental manner since the concepts which this text undertakes to explain do not alter. The areas particularly affected by new technology and new practice concern input/output, computer systems, applications, and social issues, and appropriate amendments have been incorporated to present our readers with the current scene.

We take this opportunity of thanking our editors at Prentice-Hall International for their enthusiasm in encouraging this revision.

R.H.
J.S.
1979

Preface
TO THE FIRST EDITION

In 1970, in order to meet the demands of many teachers throughout the country, and as a part of the Imperial College (London) Schools Computing Project, the authors designed an in-service course in computer appreciation for presentation at the College. During the next four years, it was repeated many times and, as a result of student feedback, the structure and emphasis were modified. In this volume, the lecture notes from the course, together with additional background material, have been collected together in the hope that they may be of use to a much wider audience.

There are many people today in commerce, industry and the professions who, without a mathematical or technical bias, are increasingly affected by computers. Indeed, many non-specialists now find themselves involved in the input and output of computer information as well as its interpretation. We believe that this introductory text will also be of benefit to those outside of education, whether in libraries, offices, government, or wherever the computer is now so widely applied.

We are grateful to many members of the Imperial College Computer Centre for their support and encouragement in the development of this book and, in particular, we would like to express our gratitude to Peter Whitehead for inspiring us to undertake this work; to Arthur Spirling for contributing some of the technical material; to Edward James for his enthusiastic support and helpful advice; and to Frances Cronin for her patient secretarial assistance throughout the preparation of the manuscript.

We would also like to thank our publishers, Prentice-Hall International, for their continued confidence. We are appreciative of the tireless diligence and good humour of Ronald Decent and Alfred Waller, who provided the editorial and production skills which have made this book a reality. Any mistakes which escaped their scrutiny are our own.

In addition, we would like to acknowledge Mr S.G.W. Nordanholt, Director of the Imperial College Computer Centre for his permission to cite the IBM 7094 system once in use at the College; the International Federation for Information Processing (IFIP) for graciously allowing us to make use of part of I.L. Auerbach's paper given at the 1962 IFIP Congress; and, finally, IBM United Kingdom Limited for permission to reproduce one of their punched cards.

R.H.
J.S.

Introduction

Computing is now an everyday term in our language. Computers are referred to in the press, on the radio and TV, and they appear in films and books — with and without an aura of science fiction. But what do they mean, to you? Some people may be exhilarated at the prospect of a computerized society, others may be despondent; some may be sceptical, and many may be cheerfully indifferent to the whole subject. These attitudes may apply to any topic which seems specialized and about which we know little, and which thereby acquires a certain mystique. We may know little, for example, about medicine or the law, but these are older disciplines and methods have been evolved (generally known or easily available to those who need them) by which we can find the right person to give us the right advice. But computers are *new* and for all their apparent complexity they seem to have a wide range cf uses and are playing an ever-increasing role within our society. So, where does one find out about them?

It is the aim of this book to remove the mystique that may surround the subject. We shall do so by trying to answer three basic questions. What is a computer? What can it do? How can one communicate with it? The concepts to be outlined will not make you an expert but, we hope, will provide sufficient background in the fundamental principles to enable you to think sensibly and talk intelligently about computing, and to show you where more specialized information, should you need it, can be found. You should be able to see the fallacies in such head-lines as "Computer makes firm bankrupt" and "Computer kills 80-year-old woman" and be able to think through what might have happened, how, and by whom. We hope that you will be able, when watching films and TV, to see through the technical charade of whirring tapes and winking lights so that you can better evaluate that which is probable and that which is fanciful. If this book provides the means whereby you can, in Darwinian terms, 'survive', that is, adapt to, and *successfully* adapt to, the computerized society, then we shall have achieved our objective.

1) "What is a computer?" This entails a definition of computing as well as a discussion about the basic anatomy of computers, their powers and limitations. This leads on to the present-day situation in which computers are often 'hidden' from the general user within computer 'systems' and their operating 'software'. Chapters 1, 2, 6 and 10 are related to this first concept.

2) "What can they do?" We consider the uses and/or applications of computers. Various issues raised by present and possible future applications are discussed. Related to this second concept are chapters 7, 8, 9 and 11.

3) "How does man communicate with computers?" This covers two broad aspects. Because of structural differences (the neurological mismatch) between man and machines, we need to 'communicate' with machines via special, though restricted, 'languages'. What programming languages are, and how they are used to instruct machines, is introduced in chapters 4 and 5. The second aspect is that of the input-output devices, those parts of the machine which convert information from the real world of man into formats which can be handled by computers. Chapter 3 covers this aspect.

The text contains the essential material relevant to these three concepts. As the *applications* of the concepts increase in sophistication, it sometimes becomes necessary to stop and develop a particular topic so that its relationship to other, subsequent, elements can be appreciated. The sequence of chapters takes this into account and the logic of the structure of the book will become more apparent as you work through it. Additional background information and technical details are included in appendices. We have tried to eliminate jargon as much as possible. Definitions are given where necessary and a Glossary and List of Acronyms are included at the end of the book, together with a Bibliography of further readings and an index.

1

An Introduction to Computing

Why Was the Computer Invented?

Many of the routine activities in today's society are being performed by computers. For example, when we go on holiday our plane seats are often reserved by computers; the traffic in some major cities is to a degree controlled by computers; the egg which you might have had for breakfast may have been laid (no, not by a computer!) by a chicken whose life history is on record on a computer file; many of the bills we pay (rates, gas, electricity, telephone, insurance, etc.) are calculated and printed by a computer. Why? And how?

It was outlined in the Introduction that there are three essential concepts that we need to examine in order to be able to think sensibly and talk intelligently about computing — What are computers? What can they do? How can we 'communicate' with them? But first of all, what do the terms *computer* and *computing* mean?

The Concise Oxford Dictionary, for once, does not help much. In the fourth edition (1950), there is only a reference to the word 'compute' meaning 'to reckon'. In the fifth edition (1964) the word 'computer' is merely defined as an 'electronic calculating machine'. This is too vague for our purposes. Obviously computing has *something* to do with reckoning or calculation, but man has been using his brain to do just that for centuries. The Egyptians built the pyramids; whoever built Stonehenge left a calendar which can still accurately predict eclipses; the Romans designed and built long straight roads, aqueducts and heating systems; early explorers navigated the globe, and even radio and television were invented — all without a computer! What is so special about them that we need computers today? It cannot simply be because they are calculating devices. We have many forms of such devices — the abacus (still used in the Far East), pocket and desk calculators, even supermarket check-out tills — all of which are cheaper and easier to use than computers. So why was the computer invented?

Because it had to be! The pressures of World War II dictated research in many areas. The new use of night bombers, submarines, and long range guns on ships and tanks meant that defenders had to fight back by shooting at targets they could not see. Technology, in the form of radar, was developed to locate the enemy; where he was, in which direction he was moving and how fast he was travelling. It was then necessary to aim guns so that when the shell was fired it would reach the enemy at the point to which he had moved. This could not be done with any accuracy without first performing detailed mathematical calculations. Firing tables were required by the men at the front line so that the figures were immediately available. But these figures were not in existence because the human effort involved in producing them was too great. What was needed was a machine which could produce the tables with the required speed and accuracy. Huge sums of money and brainpower were combined to produce the technology. In 1942, the Ballistic Research Laboratory of the U.S. Army Ordnance Department began work with the Moore School of Electrical Engineering. As a result, a computer named ENIAC had a formal dedication ceremony on 15th February, 1946.[1] ENIAC was able to produce the tables by carrying out the huge number of calculations involved, accurately and to the required precision and, because it was electronic, at a speed which made it all possible.

The problems which early computers had to solve were mostly mathematical. Today, computers are used to forecast the weather, to operate machines to cut shapes out of sheet metal, and even to guide spacecraft to the moon. They can set and print newspapers and books. They can be used to help in diagnosing diseases and to find out whether a hospital bed is available for a particular patient. They are used to find obscure documents in archives and elusive criminals on the run. Travel agents around the world have come to rely on them to book seats on air flights or rooms in hotels, either today or a year from now. Companies use them for accounting, invoicing, stock control and payrolls.[2]

The original objective for inventing the computer was to create a fast calculating machine. But in over 80% of computing today, the applications are of a non-mathematical or non-numerical nature.

To define a computer merely as a calculating device is to ignore over 80% of its work, rather like someone refusing to believe that the bulk of the iceberg lies hidden under the water. If not as a calculating device, then how are we to define a computer?

If we return to the brief list of applications above, we can discern one key fact, viz., that computers act upon information — in computing terminology, this is called 'data'. This data, or information, comes in all shapes and sizes, from a mathematical equation to the required details about a company's work force necessary to produce a payroll, or to the myriad of data needed to project an Apollo craft through space. The fact that computers process information is so fundamental, some experts have coined a word for it — *informatics,* the science of information processing, i.e., the methods of recording, manipulating and retrieving information. Many people believe this to be the essence of computing.

The Machine

Before the days of electrical engineering, attempts had been made to provide results to mathematical problems by *mechanical* means. In the early nineteenth century, Charles Babbage came closest to succeeding. At that time, mathematical and statistical tables[3] had to be compiled by small armies of clerks. Working as they did, without even the help of adding machines, the most elaborate precautions could not eliminate human errors. Babbage spent many tedious hours checking tables. From his dissatisfaction and, probably, exasperation with the clerks' inaccuracies, came the idea of a machine which could compute tables guaranteed to be error-free. Among many other achievements, Babbage designed several 'engines' as he called them, the first of these being the Difference Engine. This was built in 1822 and produced the first reliable life tables (statistics of expectation of life) which were in use for the next 50 years.

In 1833, Babbage began work on his Analytical Engine and it is this machine with which we are concerned. His requirements for precision engineering were impossible to achieve at that time and, therefore, he was unable to produce a working model of the complete, and massive, machine. Had he done so, it would have been the forerunner of today's electronic computer. But notes and drawings describe what he had in mind. The Analytical Engine was intended to be completely automatic. It was to be capable of performing the basic arithmetical functions for *any* mathematical problem and it was to do so at a speed of 60 additions a minute. The machine was to consist of five parts:

— a STORE in which to hold numbers, i.e., those which were to provide the information (data) for the problems, and those which were to be generated during the course of calculations.

— an ARITHMETIC unit which Babbage called the 'Mill'. This was to be a device for performing the arithmetical operations on the numbers which had been stored. All the operations were to have been carried out automatically through rotations of gears and wheels.

— a CONTROL unit for seeing that the machine performed the desired operations in the correct sequence and, also by means of a series of

---

1. See appendix 1, 'The Development of Computers'.
2. See chapter 7, 'Computer Applications'.
3. For insurance or actuarial (risk or probability calculations) purposes and government records.

gears and wheels, for transferring data between the Mill and the Store.

-- an INPUT device to pass into the machine both numbers (the data) and instructions as to which of the arithmetical operations to perform.

— an OUTPUT device to display the results obtained from the calculations.

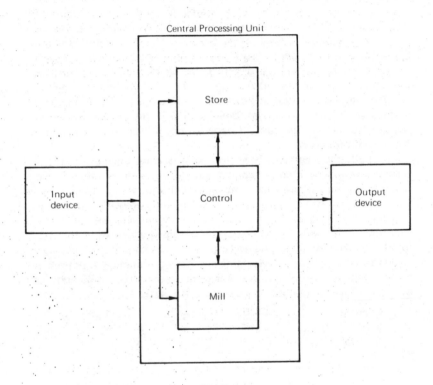

Fig. 1.1

Figure 1.1. shows these five parts in an arrangement which closely resembles the basic anatomy of today's computer. The three parts consisting of the Store, Mill and Control units are collectively known, in current terminology, as the Central Processing Unit (CPU).[4] It is this to which we really refer when talking about the computer. The other two units, the Input and Output devices (I/O),[5] are concerned with entering information (instructions and data) into the CPU, and with outputting the results once processing has taken place.

Information in the Computer

Whereas the Analytical Engine of Charles Babbage was to have been mechanical, today's computers are *electronic*. We do not define the term electronic in this book, but its use in defining the computer as an electronic calculating machine implies a machine in which all information is indicated by one of two states; either an electrical pulse is present or it is absent. For an electronic computer to be able to store our everyday, *written* characters, it has to be able to identify them as *patterns of electrical pulses.*[6] For the moment, try to visualize a sort of morse code where the dots and dashes are replaced by the *presence* or *absence* of an electrical charge. If the presence is indicated by 1 and the absence by 0 (zero), and, if the pattern 000 means S and the pattern 111 means 0, the distress signal SOS (...———...) would then appear as 000111000.

The 1's and 0's are known as *binary digits*, or **bits**.[7] The number of symbols which can be encoded will depend upon the number of signals that one allows for each symbol. If one were to allow 6 bits per symbol, one could encode up to 64 *different* symbols because six bits can be arranged in 64 unique ways.[8] It doesn't matter if you do not understand why at this particular point, provided that you can accept that the more bits you have, then the more different symbols you can encode. You should also be able to appreciate that with 64 patterns, it is possible to encode not only the 26 letters of the alphabet and the 10 decimal digits, but also up to 28 special symbols to include punctuation marks, mathematical and monetary signs.

We have said that the essential point about computers is that they process information, and we have looked, briefly, at how information is represented in the computer. Our task, now, is to consider the *nature* of this information. As human beings, we continuously make value judgements about the information we receive and instinctively process. A particular piece of art, whether a painting, piece of music or whatever, will attract some people and it may bore or even repel others. Our judgement of it will be based on our feelings, taste, knowledge and experience. But computers cannot make such judgements. They are devoid of emotions. A computer can be programmed (made) to generate poetry or music, but it cannot appraise it or judge its quality. Computers have no 'feelings' and no 'instincts'. They are machines and whilst one can build into them the equivalent of a 'memory', one cannot build into them the equivalent of a 'heart'. The human brain

4. Discussed in greater detail in chapter 2.
5. See chapter 3.
6. Elaborated in chapter 2.
7. Words appearing in **bold-face type** are more fully described in the Glossary.
8. See figure 2.2, page 16.

subconsciously acquires certain *priorities* (in the sense of making choices or determining selections based on experience, taste and individual needs). A computer cannot. It has to be consciously programmed *to follow our chosen priorities*. Computers can help mankind but they do not threaten it. They are as good only as man makes and uses them.

Computers 'approach' their information in a restricted or logical manner.[9] If any one complete task is capable of being reduced to a series of simple (individual), logical operations, then it can be performed by a computer and much more quickly than we could do it. Much of the work currently carried out by humans *is* of a logical nature and it is this which accounts for the ever growing list of computer applications rather than, as some may imagine, the 'power-lust' of the computer itself. If, for example, you analyse what is involved in driving an underground train or in assembly-line work, you will find that much of it is essentially logical (i.e., series of sequential, separate steps). Programmers, the people who are responsible for instructing computers, are therefore required to demonstrate *logical* rather than mathematical abilities. To grasp the point that the computer is a logical machine is to help put computers in their correct perspective and to show more clearly those areas where the computer is *not* in competition with man.[10]

Finally, it is important to appreciate that once a computer has been given a piece of information, it is always capable of 'remembering' it at any time. In this sense, it is far superior to a human being. Although we assimilate much information during our daily lives, we sometimes have difficulty in remembering particular things (names, places, dates, etc.) just when we need them. The computer, however, can always access (find) any piece of information that it has in store, and this data can be reproduced tomorrow, or in years to come, exactly in its original form — providing that nobody has deliberately changed it.

Input/Output Devices

The function of the I/O devices is to get information into, and out of, the CPU. We could use binary digits and make a device which would send an electrical pulse through the memory unit when it sensed a 1 bit, and not send a pulse when it did not sense a 1 bit (i.e., binary 0). Some of the first programmers did just that. The input device was then a very simple machine, but it made life very difficult for the programmer because it is not always easy to think only in terms of 1's and 0's. Developments soon led to more complex devices which can *translate* into binary patterns those characters and symbols which are familiar to us in everyday life.

A company preparing its payroll will have certain information about each worker, e.g., his name, number, department, gross pay, tax concessions, etc.

BILL BROWN, 007, GENERAL OFFICE DEPT., GROSS PAY
£XXX, TAX £YYY . . .

Each of the above characters — the letters of the alphabet, the numbers, full stop, comma and the £ symbol — can only be represented internally (in the CPU) by unique (individual) binary patterns. If Bill Brown were to get his pay slip in binary he would not be able to read it. The output from the computer must, therefore, also be in a human readable form. The input devices translate the characters *into* binary, and the output devices *re*translate them back into the familiar characters that Bill Brown can recognize. The purpose of the I/O devices is to act as translating devices between our external world and the internal world of the CPU, i.e., they act as an **interface** between man and the machine.

CHARACTERISTICS OF COMPUTERS

1) Speed: The computer was invented as a high-speed calculator. This has led to many scientific projects which were previously impossible. The control of the moon landing would not have been feasible without computers, and neither would today's more *scientific* approach to weather prediction. If we want tomorrow's forecast today (and not in six months time) meteorologists can use the computer to perform quickly the necessary calculations and analyses. When making flight reservations we want to know well in advance of take-off that a seat will be available — if it is not, then we have time to make other arrangements. The ability to get answers fast enough so that one has time to take action on them (or to make alternative plans, as in the case of airline reservations) makes **real-time** computing possible and this is discussed in chapter 6.

Electrical pulses *travel* rather than *move* at incredible speeds and, because the computer is electronic (and not tied down to mechanical movements, turning of wheels, slipping of clutches and gears), its internal speed is virtually instantaneous. We do not talk in terms of seconds or even, today, of milliseconds (thousandths of a second). Our units of speed are the microsecond (millionths), the nanosecond (thousand-millionths) and, latterly, even the picosecond (million-millionths). A powerful computer like the CDC 6600[11] is capable of

9. See chapter 4 on 'Flowcharting'.
10. See also chapter 11.
11. Each computer has its own cryptic name — CDC STAR, IBM 370, ICL 2980, even LARC (Livermore Atomic Research Computer) and LEO (Lyons' Electronic Office). See Appendix 1 and the List of Acronyms.

adding together two 18-digit numbers in 300 to 400 nanoseconds (i.e., about 3 million calculations per second).

Consider two examples from non-numerical environments. The manual indexing of the complete works of Thomas Aquinas (approximately 13 million words) would have taken 50 scholars about 40 years to accomplish. With the aid of a computer a few scholars did it in less than one year. Fingerprint identification, in time to catch a criminal before he flees the country, would be impossible without computers. The first example enables us to enjoy knowledge that would otherwise be unobtainable within our own lifetime. In the second example, the police gain time in which to act.

2) Storage: The speed with which computers can process large quantities of information has led to the generation of new information on a vast scale, in other words, the computer has compounded the information 'explosion'. How can people cope with it? We can't, but computers can. But where do they keep it all?

As a human acquires new knowledge, the brain subconsciously selects what it feels to be important and worth retaining in its memory, and relegates unimportant details to the back of the mind or just forgets them. In computers, the internal memory of the CPU is only large enough to retain a certain amount of information (i.e., it has finite limits). It is, therefore, impossible to store inside the computer the records, for example, of every Premium Bond and the names and addresses of their owners. All of this data is stored outside of the memory of the CPU, on *auxiliary* or *secondary* storage devices.[12] Small sections of the total data can be accessed (got at) very quickly by the CPU and brought into the main, internal memory, as and when required for processing.

The internal memory (in the CPU) is built up in 1K or K modules, where K equals 1024 storage locations.[13] Babbage's Analytical Engine would have been capable of holding 1000 numbers, each of 50 digits. (This compares well with many of today's *mini*-computers.) Computers come in many sizes and a small computer, such as the IBM SYSTEM/3 (model 6) has an 8K to 16K store whilst a large computer, such as the CDC CYBER 73, has up to a 128K store (i.e., 128 x 1024 locations).

3) Accuracy: In spite of misleading newspaper headlines ("Computer demands account for £0.0 to be settled immediately"), the computer's accuracy is consistently high. Errors in the machinery can occur but, due to increased efficiency in error-detecting techniques, these seldom lead to false results. Almost without exception, the errors in computing are due to human rather than to technological weaknesses, i.e., to imprecise thinking within the programming, or to inaccurate data, or to poorly designed systems.[14]

4) Versatility: Computers seem capable of performing almost any task, provided that the task can be reduced to a series of logical steps. For example, a task such as preparing a payroll or controlling the flow of traffic can be broken down into a logical sequence of operations, whereas comparing the tones of a Turner with a Vermeer cannot. Yet the computer itself has only limited ability and, in the final analysis, actually performs only *four* basic operations:

— it passes information between itself and the external world via I/O devices;
— it moves data internally within the CPU;
— it performs the basic arithmetical operations;
— it performs operations of comparison.[15]

In one sense, then, the computer is not versatile because it is limited to four basic functions. Yet, because so many daily activities can be reduced to an interplay between these functions, it appears that computers are highly ingenious. Programming[16] is the craft of reducing a given problem into an interplay between these few operations.

5) Automatic: A computer is much more than an adding machine, calculator or check-out till, all of which require human operators to press the necessary keys for the operations to be performed. Once a program is in the computer's memory, the individual instructions are then transferred, one after the other, to the control unit for execution. The CPU follows these instructions ('do this', 'do that', 'do the other', etc.) until it meets a last instruction which says 'stop program execution'. When Babbage claimed that his Analytical Engine would be *automatic,* he meant that once the process had begun, it would continue *without the need for human intervention* until completion.

6) Diligence: Being a machine, a computer does not suffer from the human traits of tiredness and lack of concentration. If 3 million calculations have to be performed, it will perform the 3 millionth with *exactly* the same accuracy and speed as the first. This factor may cause those whose jobs are highly repetitive to regard the computer as a threat. But to those who rely on a continuous standard of output, e.g., quality control in the refining of oil and other chemical processes, the computer will be seen as a considerable help.

* * *

12. Usually, magnetic tape or disks. See chapter 3.
13. See chapter 2, page 24.
14. See chapters 4,5,9.
15. See also chapter 5.
16. See chapters 4 and 5.

We began by pointing out some of the uses of computers. We conclude this chapter with a quotation that aptly underlines their significance:

"Yesterday people questioned our ability to build a digital[17] computer. Today the computer has already shown that it is one of man's great tools, and that its potential benefits for mankind are tremendous. But these benefits are not inevitable; nor are they unmitigated. We will have to work hard to realize the benefits fully. The entire world will have to plan carefully to avoid the dangers that accompany progress.

It is important for us to remember — and for the rest of the world to realize — that the computer has begun an information revolution that will profoundly affect the lives of everyone. I realize that these are strong words. Not everyone will agree that the changes in progress are actually revolutionary. But the computer and modern information processing techniques do far more than amplify man's physical force, which was the basis of the industrial revolution. These tools amplify man's ability to manipulate information. This amplification will cause revisions in our economic, government, and social structures as drastic as the ones caused by the industrial revolution."[18]

*   *   *

We have looked at the meaning of computing, analyzed the basic structure of the computer, and discussed its characteristics. We shall now extend our examination more deeply as follows:

Chapter 2   looks at the basic anatomy and structure in more detail;

Chapter 3   investigates the various I/O devices which interface between the CPU and the real world of man, and considers auxiliary storage media;

Chapters 4 & 5   discuss programming, and modes of communication between men and computers (computer 'languages');

Chapter 6   expands our view of the basic machine to consider it more properly as, and within, a computer *system;*

Chapter 7   looks at some of the many uses to which computers are applied;

Chapters 8 & 9   investigate the concepts of information *structuring* and the preparations necessary for computer processing of data;

Chapter 10   outlines the organization and personnel required to operate a computer installation;

Chapter 11   discusses the implications for society of the computer.

17. digital = of digits or numbers. See also chapter 2, opening paragraph.
18. "The Impact of Information Processing on Mankind", I.L. Auerbach, *Information Processing '62*, Popplewell, Editor, North-Holland Publishing. Journal of International Federation for Information Processing (IFIP).

2

The Basic Anatomy of the Computer

A reference has been made to a *digital* computer. By inference, the digital machine is one which operates essentially by counting (using information, including letters and other symbols, in coded form represented by two-state electronic components). This is in contrast to the *analogue* computer which operates by measuring rather than by counting. The analogue machine, because it has only a limited memory facility and is restricted in the type of calculations it can perform, can only be used for certain specialized engineering and scientific applications. Most computers are digital. Indeed, the word 'computer' is generally accepted as being synonymous with the term 'digital computer'.

Basic Structure

Remembering Babbage's Analytical Engine, let us see what happens in a computer. It receives information (input); it processes this information in some way according to a set of precise instructions (in the CPU); and it then presents the results in a useful form (output).

On closer inspection we find that the CPU (the computer itself, remember) has to store the information in a memory before it can carry out any processing operations. Two kinds of information have to be input, the program and the data. The program is the set of instructions which the computer is to carry out, and the data is the information on which these instructions are to operate. For example, if the task is to sort a list of telephone subscribers into alphabetical order, the sequence of instructions or procedure which guides the computer through this operation is the program, whilst the list of names to be sorted is the data.

In the Analytical Engine calculations were to be handled by an arithmetic unit which Babbage called the Mill. The computer also has an arithmetic unit. Arithmetic, because *all* computer operations involve the manipulation of numbers. All information, program and data, are represented in numeric form (bit patterns). The manipulations also include making comparisons and logic type operations[1] as well as

12

arithmetical operations (+ − x ÷), and for this reason the unit is referred to in full as the Arithmetic and Logic Unit (ALU).

In order to insure that information is correctly placed in store, and that the program instructions are followed in the proper sequence and data is selected from memory as necessary, a control unit is required.

The control unit, together with the ALU and memory unit, form the Central Processing Unit (CPU). The following diagram differs from fig. 1.1 only in that the Mill has now become the ALU and the word 'memory' has been used instead of 'store' (the two being synonymous).

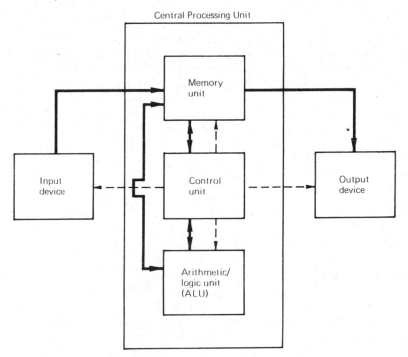

Fig. 2.1 Basic Structure of the Computer

However, with the different use of arrows we can indicate the flow of information (full lines) and the control of events (dotted lines), and extend our appreciation of the significance and role of the control unit.

The program instructions and data are transferred, *under the direction of the control unit,* from the input device into the memory. During program execution, each instruction is retrieved in turn (proper sequence) from the memory and interpreted. Control informs the ALU of the precise operation to be performed and directs the transfer to the

1. The significance of comparisons and logic type operations is developed in
   chapters 4 and 5.

ALU of any item of data which is needed for the operation. The ALU then executes all calculations and comparisons. Results destined for output are then passed to memory where they are held in storage temporarily, prior to presentation by the output device. This procedure also takes place under the direction of the control unit.

A Clerical Exercise

Suppose you need to compare the number who passed with the number who failed; or the range of marks (highest to lowest) of all the candidates, or only of those who passed, or only of those who failed; or the average mark; or how many were above these averages and how many below them. You need to know what is required now, and what may be needed later, before you can devise the best way to proceed, in a series of strictly logical and separate steps.

Try to think of ways in which you can gather as much information as possible during one detailed check through the papers, and of how this information can be sorted in the several ways you need, without having to re-check through the papers again and again. This is what a programmer would have to do if he was seeking a computer solution to the problem. The formal way he would set about this involves using *flowcharts,* the principles of which are explained in chapter 4.

DATA REPRESENTATION WITHIN THE COMPUTER

Information is handled in the computer by electrical components such as **transistors** and **integrated circuits, magnetic cores** and **semiconductors,** and wires, all of which can only indicate two states or conditions. Transistors are either conducting or non-conducting; magnetic materials are either magnetized or non-magnetized, or magnetized in one direction or in the opposite direction; a pulse or voltage is present or not present. All information is represented within the computer by the presence or absence of these various signals. The binary number system, which has only two digits, zero (0) and one (1), is conveniently used to express the two possible states.

All the familiar symbols which we use in *written* information are represented in the computer by *combinations of bits* (a unique pattern for each symbol). A 'set' of such combinations of bits would include the letters of the alphabet, the digits $0 \rightarrow 9$, and certain special characters such as punctuation marks. A set containing all these characters is known as an 'alphanumeric (or alphameric) character set'. A common method of coding is to use a combination of six bits for each character. Since six bits can be arranged in 64 different ways, this allows for a 64-character set (see fig. 2.2). Five bits per symbol would only provide 32 possible permutations and this would be insufficient for the number of characters we need to represent.

Computer 'Words'

We express information in *words.* So do many computers. A computer 'word' is a group of bits, the length of which varies from

Decimal Number	The Binary Equivalent represented by six bits	Character represented	Decimal Number	The Binary Equivalent represented by six bits	Character represented
0	0 0 0 0 0 0	none	32	1 0 0 0 0 0	5
1	0 0 0 0 0 1	A	33	1 0 0 0 0 1	6
2	0 0 0 0 1 0	B	34	1 0 0 0 1 0	7
3	0 0 0 0 1 1	C	35	1 0 0 0 1 1	8
4	0 0 0 1 0 0	D	36	1 0 0 1 0 0	9
5	0 0 0 1 0 1	E	37	1 0 0 1 0 1	+
6	0 0 0 1 1 0	F	38	1 0 0 1 1 0	—
7	0 0 0 1 1 1	G	39	1 0 0 1 1 1	*
			40	1 0 1 0 0 0	/
	Patterns representing H ⟶ R		41	1 0 1 0 0 1	(
			42	1 0 1 0 1 0	)
			43	1 0 1 0 1 1	£
			44	1 0 1 1 0 0	.
19	0 1 0 0 1 1	S			
20	0 1 0 1 0 0	T			
21	0 1 0 1 0 1	U			
22	0 1 0 1 1 0	V		Patterns representing additional special characters	
23	0 1 0 1 1 1	W			
24	0 1 1 0 0 0	X			
25	0 1 1 0 0 1	Y			
26	0 1 1 0 1 0	Z			
27	0 1 1 0 1 1	0			
28	0 1 1 1 0 0	1			
29	0 1 1 1 0 1	2			
30	0 1 1 1 1 0	3	62	1 1 1 1 1 0	→
31	0 1 1 1 1 1	4	63	1 1 1 1 1 1	>

Fig. 2.2 Part of an imaginary 64-character set (each character represented by 6 bits). The special characters have particular significance within the use of the various programming languages.

machine to machine, but it is predetermined for each machine. The word length may be as long as 60 bits or as short as 8 bits.[2]

Information is made up of data and program (instructions). It is stored in the form of alphanumeric data, numeric data, or as machine instructions. We shall see that in each case the computer word is arranged differently. Let us consider a 36-bit word and see how it

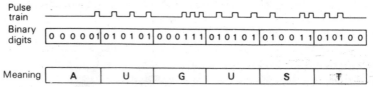

Fig. 2.3 Six alphanumeric characters, viz., the bit pattern representation of "AUGUST" stored in one 36-bit word. The code used is the same one that we built up in fig. 2.2. The wavy line above is to indicate the relationship between a 'train' of pulses (how the information is moved about in the machine) and the string of bits it represents. The string is shown with equal spaces between the pulses. The presence of a pulse indicates a 1 bit and the absence of a pulse a 0 bit.

relates to the alphanumeric coding. If the alphanumeric data is grouped into 6-bit patterns, one word would contain six characters (fig.2.3).

Numeric data on the other hand uses the entire word since groups of 6-bits would severely restrict the size of numbers. In order to grasp this point fully we must be clear about counting in binary.

Number Systems

A number is made up of individual digits (e.g., 803 consists of the digits 8, 0 and 3). The value of each digit in a number is determined by three considerations:

1) the digit itself;
2) the position of the digit in the number;
3) the base of the number system (where base is defined as the number of digits which can occur in any one position).

In the decimal system the base is equal to 10 since any position can contain one of ten digits (0 1 2 3 4 5 6 7 8 9). The system therefore has a carrying factor of 10 and each digit indicates a value which depends on the position it occupies:

In   6,421 the digit 6 signifies 6 x 1000
     4,621   6 x 100
     4,261   6 x 10
     4,216   6

Binary Number System

In binary the base is equal to 2 and the two digits are 0 and 1. As we have seen, this system is ideal for coding purposes for the computer because of the two-state nature of the electrical components which are used.

Binary Counting

Remember we only have two digits, 0 and 1, and therefore the binary equivalent of the decimal number 2 has to be stated as 10 (a zero with a 1 carry, read as 'one, zero').

2. In some computers the fundamental grouping of bits is called a byte rather than a word. A byte is usually shorter than a word, typically consisting of eight bits. An eight-bit byte can for example be used to represent one alphanumeric character or two decimal digits. In other computers the grouping of bits, bytes or words is flexible in design to meet the differing storage requirements of numbers, alphanumeric characters and instructions.

Binary	Decimal Equivalent
0	0
1	1
10	2
11	3
100	4
101	5
110	6
111	7
1000	8
1001	9
1010	10
1011	11
1100	12
1101	13
1110	14
1111	15

This system has a carrying factor of 2 and each bit has a value which depends on the position it occupies:

In binary 1011

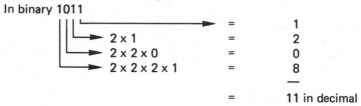

	=	1
2 x 1	=	2
2 x 2 x 0	=	0
2 x 2 x 2 x 1	=	8
	=	11 in decimal

In our 36-bit word, numeric data can be represented by up to 35 bits with the 36th bit always reserved to indicate whether the number is positive or negative.

Numbering the bit positions from the right, we can assign each bit a value based on 2 times the value of the previous bit. The number 1,208, 747 is represented in the computer by the unique pattern of 1's and 0's illustrated in fig. 2.4. It is the total value of those bits (reading from right to left) marked with a 1, i.e.,

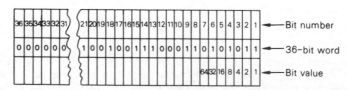

Fig. 2.4 A positive number stored in a 36-bit word. A zero sign in bit 36 indicates a positive number, a one sign a negative number.

Bit No		Value	
	1		1
	2		2
	4		8
	6		32
	8		128
	9		256
	13		4096
	14		8192
	15		16384
	18		131072
	21		1048576

$$1208747$$

THE ARITHMETIC AND LOGIC UNIT

This handles both the arithmetic and logical operations on which much of a computer program is based. Before we can think about how circuitry could be designed to handle these functions, we need to have some knowledge of the simplicity of the arithmetic involved.

Computer Arithmetic

Addition: We have pointed out how numbers are counted in binary and that numbers are made up of bit patterns only of 1's and 0's. When adding these digits together the result will also be in 1's and 0's. The following examples indicate all possible combinations of 0 and 1 for addition:

```
  0      0      1      1
 +0     +1     +0     +1
 ──     ──     ──     ──
  0      1      1     10
```

Note that the sum of 1 and 1 is written as '10' (a zero sum with a 1 carry) which is the equivalent of the decimal digit '2'.

We can now look at three examples of binary additions which make use of the above combinations:

	Binary	*Decimal Equivalent*
Ex. 1	1 0 1 0	10
	+ 1 0 1	+ 5
	───────	──
	1 1 1 1	15

	Binary	*Decimal Equivalent*
carry	1	carry 1
Ex. 2	1 0 1 0 1 0	42
	+ 1 0 0 1	+ 9
	───────────	───
	1 1 0 0 1 1	51

	Binary	*Decimal Equivalent*
carry	1 1 1	carry 11
Ex. 3	1 0 1 1 1 0 0 0	184
	+ 1 1 1 0 1 1	+ 59
	─────────────	───
	1 1 1 1 0 0 1 1	243

In the third example we find a new situation (1+1+1) brought about by the 1 carry. However, we can still handle this by using the four combinations already mentioned. We add the digits in turn. 1 + 1 = 10 (a zero sum with a 1 carry). The third 1 is now added to this result to obtain 11 (a 1 sum with a 1 carry).

Our sums have been set down in the traditional manner for human solution. They do not show how the computer adds but they do illustrate the combinations of 1's and 0's that the computer circuitry will have to handle.

The computer performs *all* the other arithmetical operations (x − ÷) by a form of addition. This is easily seen in the case of multiplication, e.g., 9 x 5 may be thought of as essentially being determined by evaluating, with necessary carry overs, 9+9+9+9+9. This idea of repeated addition may seem to be a longer way of doing things, but remember that the computer is well suited to carry out the operation at great speed. Subtraction and division are handled essentially by addition using the principle of *complementing*.

Complementary Subtraction: The computer performs *all* mathematical operations by a form of addition. How can subtraction be achieved using an essentially additive method? The shopkeeper knows how because he does so every time he gives you change. In order to find the right amount of change he merely complements the cost of the purchase up to the sum of money you have offered him. In ordinary (decimal) arithmetic the highest number in any column (units, tens, hundreds, etc.) is 9. The 'nines complement' is that number which, when added to another, makes a total of 9, 99, 999, etc. Hence:

The nines complement of 6	of 10	of 385
is said to be 3	is 89	is 614
─	──	───
9	99	999

When subtracting by the complementary method three steps are involved:

Step 1 Find the nines complement of the number you are subtracting;
2 Add this to the number from which you are taking away;
3 Add 1 if the carry is set and 0 if it is not set; if the carry is not set recomplement to obtain the result and attach a negative sign.

Normal Subtraction

$$\begin{array}{r} 25 \\ -10 \\ \hline 15 \end{array} \qquad \begin{array}{r} 14 \\ -72 \\ \hline -58 \end{array}$$

Using Complementary Method

```
          25                              14
Step 1  +89 (nines complement of 10)    +27 (nines complement of 72)
        ───                             ───
  2     114                             041
         └─►1 (carry set, add 1)          └─►0 (carry not set, add 0)
───     ───                             ───
Result   15                              41
```

Result   −58 (recomplement and attach negative sign)

When applied to computer arithmetic the significance of this method soon becomes apparent. The binary system only has two digits, therefore subtraction involves 'ones complement.' This is simplicity itself because to obtain the complement, one merely reverses the bits of the binary number, e.g., the ones complement of 1010 is 0101.

Let us take an example to see how it works;

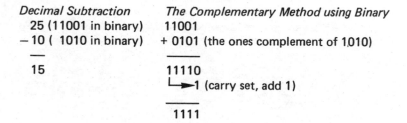

```
Decimal Subtraction          The Complementary Method using Binary
  25 (11001 in binary)       11001
− 10 ( 1010 in binary)       + 0101 (the ones complement of 1,010)
  ──                         ─────
  15                         11110
                               └─►1 (carry set, add 1)
                             ─────
                              1111
```

The computer performs the division operation essentially by repeating this complementary subtraction method, e.g. $45 \div 9$ may be thought of as $45 - 9 = 36 - 9 = 27 - 9 = 18 - 9 = 9 - 9 = 0$ (minus 9 *five* times).

We have demonstrated how computer arithmetic is based on addition. Exactly how this simplifies matters can only be understood in the context of binary (not in decimal). The number of individual steps may indeed be increased because all computer arithmetic is reduced to addition, but the computer can carry out binary additions at such great speed that this is not a disadvantage.

Arithmetic Section of the ALU

We have not considered how the computer handles fractions nor have we considered number systems, other than binary, associated with computers, e.g. **octal** (based on eight) and **hexadecimal** (based on sixteen). These two systems are significant because they provide a shorthand notion for expressing binary. Those who wish to explore these subjects should refer to the Bibliography.

To summarize the basic principles of computer arithmetic it will be seen that:

   a) all forms of arithmetic are handled by a form of addition;
   b) to do this we need to add 1's and 0's to produce other 1's and 0's.

We also need facilities for 'carrying over' and for 'reversing' (to 'complement'). It is not necessary to understand the intricacies of the electronic circuits which are designed to perform these functions, but only that the operations are carried out by means of combinations of signals passing through what are known as 'logic elements' or 'logic gates'.

Logic Gates: Circuits are built up using combinations of different types of gates to perform the necessary arithmetic. There are several types of gates, but we shall consider here only three elementary logic gates known as AND, OR and NOT. These are sufficient to introduce the concept of circuit design and to demonstrate the four possible combinations of 1 and 0 in addition.

   a) An AND gate generates an output signal of 1 only if *all* input signals are also 1.

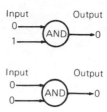

b) An OR gate generates an output signal of 1 if *any* of the input signals are also 1.

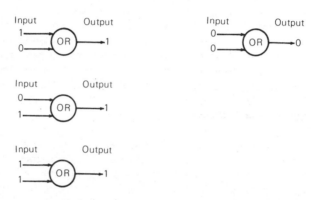

c) a NOT gate generates an output signal which is the *reverse* of the original signal.

By using the output from one gate as part of the input for another gate, and by using a variety of gates arranged in different sequences, we can build up circuitry to handle arithmetic involving 1's and 0's.

If we reconsider the four possible addition situations we see that the computer must be able to provide for:

0 + 0 to produce a 0 sum and a 0 carry
0 + 1   1 sum and a 0 carry
1 + 0   1 sum and a 0 carry
1 + 1   0 sum and a 1 carry

Our need is to produce a series of logic gates which can resolve *all four* situations correctly, so that whatever the two input signals, the correct sum is always obtained as well as the correct carry (i.e. the *one* circuit works for all). This can be done using two AND gates, one OR and one

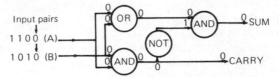

Fig. 2.5 Arrangement of gates to add any pair of bits.

NOT, combined in the design illustrated in fig 2.5. Trace any pair of inputs through from A and B and see how the sum and carry are always correct. The first pair (0,0) has been taken through the total circuit for you and the output signal at each stage indicated.

By linking together designs like this, by using other types of gates that we have not mentioned, and by using gates which can have more than two inputs, we can begin to build up complete circuits which will do all the necessary computer arithmetic operations and be able to work with large strings of bits rather than two at a time.

Logic Section of the ALU

The logic gates in the ALU which enable arithmetic to be performed should not be confused with the ability of the computer to handle (test) various conditions occurring during program execution, and to take appropriate action based on the instructions provided by the human programmer. The significance of these logical operations to programming is developed in chapters 4 and 5.

The logical section of the ALU performs all the necessary logical functions, but the details of the circuitry used are beyond the scope of this book.

MEMORY UNIT

The ALU needs data upon which to act and instructions as to how to act. These are obtained from the memory unit which is made up of a number of locations or cells. In each of these locations a word can be stored. A location, therefore, is capable of retaining either an instruction or a piece of data. The number and size of locations in a store (measured in K modules, remember) varies from machine to machine. Each is numbered sequentially to provide a unique reference for an item of information held in store. This reference is known as the *location address*.

The Purpose of Addressing

The concept of addressing is no different from the familiar method of identifying houses in a street. Each house has a number or name, or

1025	1030	1035	1040	1045	1050	1055	1060
1026	1031	1036	1041	1046	1051	1056	1061
1027	1032	1037 "AUGUST"	1042	1047	1052	1057	1062
1028	1033	1038	1043	1048	1053	1058	1063
1029	1034	1039	1044	1049	1054	1059 "1,208,747"	1064

Fig. 2.6 A matrix[3] to represent a small section (locations 1025–1064) of the memory of a hypothetical computer. The number in the top left-hand corner of each cell is the location address (the computer's method of referencing each location). The bit pattern, which according to the context of the program, can be interpreted as "AUGUST" is stored at location 1037 and the bit pattern representing "1,208,747" is stored at location 1059.

both, by which it is recognized. It is this unique reference which leads to correspondence (letters, cards, parcels) being delivered to the correct house. The purpose of addressing each location of a computer memory is to identify each cell so that an item of information may be placed in store and thereafter be traced by reference to the location address, which is 'remembered' by the computer. This means the contents of a storage location can be altered and the new information retrieved without the actual contents being known. For example, '19 High Street' is a unique address and Mr Smith may be the present occupant. If Smith leaves and Jones moves in, the postman, like the control unit of the computer, will still continue to deliver correspondence addressed to '19 High Street', irrespective of who the occupant is.

Instructions

In the clerical exercise, a comparison must be made between a student's mark and the constant pass mark. This process cannot take place in the memory. It takes place in the arithmetic and logic unit. Before considering this point further it is necessary to examine the basic format of a computer instruction.

An instruction extracted from a word of memory by the control

3. Note that the use of a 5 x 8 matrix in this example is not significant. It could just as well have been 40 x 1 or 10 x 4.

OPERATION (Code)	ADDRESS (Location)

Fig. 2.7 Computer Instruction.

unit normally consists of two parts (see fig 2.7). The operation code is present to signify what has to be done, whilst the address indicates the exact memory location which contains the information to be used when the operation is carried out (executed).

A group of instructions to perform a comparison of a student's mark with the pass mark could be described as follows:

Step 1   Move 'pass mark' and 'current student's mark' from store (memory) into the ALU;

2   Compare these two marks;

3a   If 'student's mark' is less than 'pass mark' then ignore this mark and move to next 'student's mark';

3b   If 'student's mark' is equal to, or greater than, 'pass mark' then add 'student's name and mark' to 'pass list'.

The instructions have been explained in English, of course. In the computer, the instructions have to be defined by *numeric* codes since, as we have seen, all information ends up internally in numeric form.

056	0014

Fig. 2.8 Computer Instruction.

Fig 2.8 illustrates this, but we have used ordinary (decimal) numbers rather than binary for convenience.

If the interpretation of *operation code* 056 is 'add', the example simply states 'add (to the accumulator; see *Registers)* the contents of location address 0014' which, remember, is the *location* of the information, not the information itself.[4]

CONTROL UNIT

It is part of the function of the control unit, once it receives an instruction involving either a calculation or a comparison, to control the movement of data into the ALU and, once the operation has been completed, to move the result to a specified storage location.

If we summarize the computing process we find that the control unit is designed to co-ordinate the representation, storage, and internal movement of instructions and data, as well as the interpretation and subsequent execution of those instructions, and it then has to pass on the results.

Registers

We have noted that there is movement of information within the CPU as each instruction is interpreted and executed. To handle this process satisfactorily it is necessary, at various stages, to retain information on a temporary basis. To do this, the computer uses a number of special memory units called *registers*. They are not considered part of the main memory, and there are several types of register, each designed to perform a specific function. What they have in common is the ability to receive information, to hold it temporarily, and to pass it on as directed by the control unit.

| STORAGE | register holds information on its way to and from memory.

| INSTRUCTION | register holds an instruction whilst it is being executed.

| ADDRESS | register holds a storage location address until it is needed.

| ACCUMULATOR | register accumulates results.

* * *

We hope that, in your brain, your human 'registers' have been at work and that the relationships between the ALU, Memory and Control units (the three components of the CPU), are now apparent. We have been concerned with the concepts, the basic principles — the detailed practice of these principles, it will be seen, can soon become very complicated. If these concepts, however, are understood, we can now introduce the idea of a computer installation in which the CPU exists as the centre of all activities.

A COMPUTER INSTALLATION

We have considered the basic structure of a computer and discovered that it has five functional units. However, in reality it is not as straightforward as this. A computer needs storage space over and above the

4. These principles are discussed more fully in chapter 5.

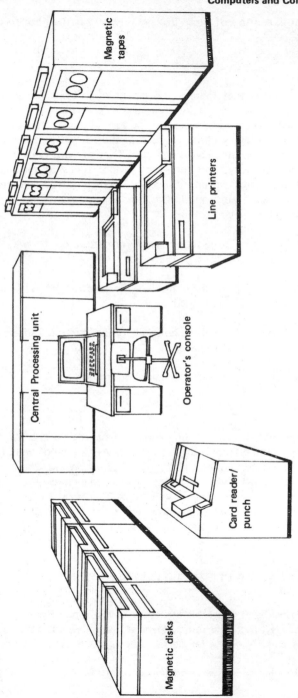

Fig. 2.9 A Computer Installation

capacity of its own memory (we recognised this fact in connection with the storage of all the Premium Bond records). The main store of a computer is designed as a working area for a program, i.e. it provides space for the instructions and data (at least for that portion of the data which is currently required), and also space for program manipulation. Information in the memory is only retained on a temporary basis (until the termination of the program). Clearly then, this area of *primary storage* is not the place for information which has to be retained permanently. An area of *secondary storage* is needed for this category of information and this is provided by such auxiliary or 'back-up' storage devices as magnetic disk and magnetic tape.

The input stage of the computing process can be handled by any one of a number of different input devices, e.g., punched card readers and teletypewriter terminals. Equally, there are a number of output devices and, of these, the line printer is the one most commonly used. A computer installation may operate using a *variety* of input/output devices. These various devices, together with back-up (secondary) storage are discussed in the next chapter.

Hardware is the jargon term given to the machinery itself and to the various individual pieces of equipment. When the hardware is linked together to form an effective working unit we have a computer installation. However, you can do nothing useful with the computer hardware on its own. It has to be driven by certain utility programs, called *software,* which are input and stored permanently in the computer system. The nature and significance of software is dealt with in chapters 5 and 6.

3
Man-Machine/Machine-Man Communication

The first electronic computer was completed in 1946, yet it was not until the mid-fifties that the computer industry was firmly established. Since that time, aided by new technology, the industry has made phenomenal progress. For example, notable advances have occurred in the provision of storage and in processor speeds. These in turn have facilitated the development of sophisticated computer systems and complex software.[1] Future developments read like a science-fiction story with powerful computers shrunk to the size of a match-box. However, there is one area which, generally speaking, has not developed to the same extent. This is in the realm of 'man-machine' and 'machine-man' communication, in other words, the input-output devices. The principal reason for this is that speed of communication depends in many cases on mechanical movement and the potential for improvement of such devices is limited.

Input-output units surround the central processor, hence the term *peripheral devices.* Their purpose is to provide an information link between the outside world and the CPU. In computing parlance, they act as an *interface,* translating the familiar symbols which we can read into the binary patterns that can be handled electronically within the CPU: they then translate the patterns back again for easily readable output.

INPUT

Communicating with computers has always been a problem. It would be marvellous if one could talk directly to a computer by normal speech, and if it could then reply in our own language. Research is, in fact, taking place in this area with interesting developments and some commercial companies are already using this method of communication in a limited way with a restricted vocabulary. However, speech recognition is not expected to become a viable input technique in the immediate future. Up to the present time, developments have taken place which permit the computer to 'read' our typed (and even 'written') symbols directly, via mark recognition (mark reading, mark sensing),

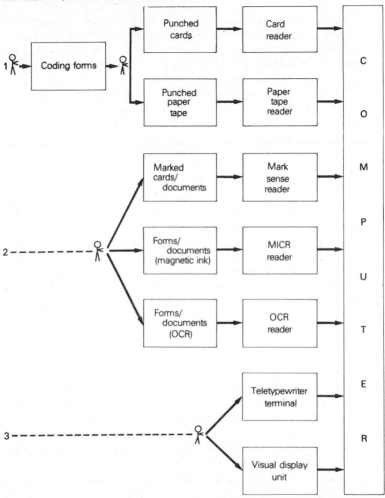

Fig. 3.1 Communication Path Diagram.

magnetic-ink character recognition (MICR) and optical character recognition (OCR). There have also been developments which have led to typewriter input (teletypewriter) devices and to visual (TV-type) display devices.

But, in the early days, programmers had to communicate directly with the computer in its own language. Man, rather than the machine, had to do the translating. The difficulties of having to think in binary

1. See chapter 6.

led man to develop easier methods of communication. In some cases he was able to do this by making use of existing technology from other fields. For example, the use of punched cards and perforated tape permitted the encoding of our familiar symbols *by people unfamiliar with binary* into an intermediate stage. This intermediate stage is then translated, *by the machine,* into binary. The diagram (Fig. 3.1) on p. 31 shows the various paths by which man can communicate with the machine. It will be noted that the number of steps by which man can input information decreases as the input device increases in sophistication.

Path 1: Punched Cards and Paper Tape

a) **Card Punching and Reading:** Punched card input using path 1 is the traditional form of communication. Today, the punched card is declining in importance though it is still of significance. It is not a new idea. As early as 1801, Joseph Jacquard built a weaving loom in which the movement of the threads was controlled by the presence and absence of holes in cards. Today's punched card is developed directly from an idea patented by Herman Hollerith in 1889. As a method of communication it is relatively easy to comprehend.

The information to be passed to the machine is normally hand-written first on *coding forms,* so that it can be easily read by the card punch operator who then transcribes this information onto cards. A card may have 40, 80 or even 96 columns, though 80 is standard. The coding form is divided into columns to match the card (only one character per column). The punch machine resembles an elaborate type-writer which punches a set of holes in a card instead of printing characters on paper.

The code for the representation of characters is examined in some

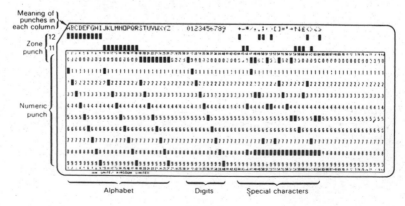

Fig. 3.2

detail to provide an example of one way that information is prepared for input to the computer. The card reader is designed to accept this code and to generate electronic pulses, representing sequences of bits which the computer can understand.

A card is divided into 12 rows and, for the purpose of defining the code, these rows are split into two groups (zone and numeric) as illustrated in Fig. 3.2. One column (containing one to three punched holes) represents one character.

Letters:	one zone punch combined with one numeric punch
Numbers:	the corresponding numeric punch only
Symbols:	one, two, or three punches depending on the particular symbol.

Character	Code	Character	Code	Character	Code
A	12−1	T	0−3	,	0−3−8
B	12−2	U	0−4	.	12−3−8
C	12−3	:	:	£	11−3−8
D	12−4	Y	0−8	*	11−4−8
:	:	Z	0−9	:	:
I	12−9	0	0		
J	11−1	1	1	/	0−1
K	11−2	2	2	=	3−8
L	11−3	3	3	+	12
:	:	4	4	−	11
R	11−9	8	8		
S	0−2	9	9		

Fig. 3.3 A Card Code. The alphabetic and numeric codes are common to all manufacturers, but there are slight variations for special symbols.

The 80 characters represented by the 80 columns could provide several words or pieces of related information. If cards are used for identifying people, for example, one might allow columns 1-10 for a person's name, columns 11-40 for the number of his house and the name of his street, columns 41-55 for the county or postal code, columns 56-65 for the country. Columns 66-80 could be used to represent other things about the person, e.g., sex, age, profession or job status, etc. The 80 columns could be allocated to describe different things, e.g., the names, numbers and types of different products, items in particular shops, factories, libraries, etc. The use of the cards in such ways would be input of data.[2] Information punched on cards is normally checked before it is input to the computer, through a process known as verification. A second operator keys in the data again using a machine which instead of cutting holes checks the characters on the cards already punched. When a mismatch occurs a possible error has

2. Cards can also be used to input instructions (the computer program).

been unearthed. Great efforts have to be made whatever method of input is in use to prevent incorrect data being fed to the computer. The interface between the punched card and the computer is the *card reader*. In the more modern readers, the card passes between a light source and a set of photo-electric cells. The presence of a hole causes the light to create a pulse by triggering one of the cells. This later method is faster. Speeds of card readers vary from 100-2000 cards per minute. Most of those connected to large computers are in the upper range, giving a maximum character transfer rate of approximately 160,000 per minute. This is impressive for a mechanical device in which the physical movement of cards is involved, but it is as well to realize that the CPU may transfer information internally a thousand times faster. (See Fig. 3.13).

b) Paper Tape Punching and Reading: Perforated paper tape had been in use for many years before the invention of the computer. It can be found on old pianola rolls and was (and still is) used by type-setters (the monotype process). The computing industry has adopted, and adapted, this technique. Computer tape is normally 1 inch wide, comes in rolls, and may be used in any length up to several hundred feet. Information is recorded as holes punched in rows across the width of the tape, with one row representing one character. The maximum number of holes in this row is referred to as the number of *channels* on the tape. An eight-channel tape is the most common. Tapes make use of different codes depending on the number of channels.

The paper tape reader operates in a similar manner to the card reader. The tape passes a reading unit where the presence or absence of holes is sensed and converted to electrical pulses. A speed of 2000 characters per second is considered a high transfer rate with typical speeds about half this rate.

Paper tape, like punched cards, is punched using a perforating machine with a keyboard. It is cheaper than cards and less bulky for storage purposes, but punched tape has the reputation of being more

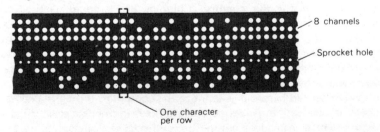

Fig. 3.4 Punched Tape — Eight-channel type. The sprocket holes run the length of the tape for the purpose of feeding the tape through the tape punching and reading device.

difficult to verify and correct. The continuous nature of the tape also means that it is more difficult to make insertions and deletions of data. However, paper tape is a versatile medium. It is used for regularly repeated, and usually small, programs, e.g. as input to printout short lists of names and addresses for labels. In addition, certain teletype-writer terminals (see page 38) use paper tape to record the input of data. Similarly paper tape attachments for recording data are associated with a number of business machines, e.g. various accounting type machines and cash registers.

Path 2: Mark and Character Recognition

This method involves the recognition of marks or characters, e.g. from work dockets, cheques, till rolls, and also cards. There are three types of recognition:

a) Mark Sense Reading
b) Magnetic Ink Character Recognition (MICR)
c) Optical Character Recognition (OCR)

On the whole, to achieve the required standard of accuracy which the computing process demands, the reading devices associated with mark and character recognition operate, so far, at slower rates than the more highly developed punched card reader.

a) **Mark Sense Reading:** This is literally what it says. The card or form is divided up into boxes, in which a mark is made by pencil or pen. A character is represented by marking the correct combination of boxes in any one column, as opposed to displacing holes from a punched card. Forms and cards are pre-printed for special purposes so that a mark can be made in a certain position to represent a YES or NO answer to a question, or to signify a number, as on insurance forms, gas and electricity recording cards.

In one form of detection, the conductivity of graphite marks is sensed. The method necessitates the use of a soft pencil, and non-graphite pen or printed marks are not acceptable. Another method uses equipment which reads marks optically. Quite simply a light source senses the presence of a mark. In this case, special pencils are not required to mark up the cards or documents.

b) **Magnetic Ink Character Recognition (MICR):** Due to the success of mark recognition, investigation turned to the possibility of *reading* characters. The first successful form of character recognition was in the area of MICR. This system uses highly stylized character shapes printed in an ink containing magnetizable particles. Early in 1966, two standard

E 13 B Font

0 1 2 3 4 5 6 7 8 9

···· I: ,' II·

C M C 7 Font

0 1 2 3 4 5 6 7 8 9

A B C D E F G H I J K L M

N O P Q R S T U V W X Y Z

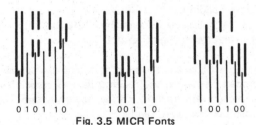

| 0 1 0 1 1 0 | 1 0 0 1 1 0 | 1 0 0 1 0 0 |

Fig. 3.5 MICR Fonts

MICR fonts (typographical styles) were accepted by the International Standards Organization. One, known as E13B, consists of the numerals 0—9 and four special characters. This is used principally for bank cheques. The code number of the bank, the customer's account number, and the cheque sequence number are all preprinted in magnetic ink. When a cheque is submitted to a bank, the amount of the transaction is enscribed on it before the cheque is presented for computer processing.

The magnetized ink induces a current in a reading circuit. The current induced will be proportional to the area of ink being scanned. The patterns of the varying currents can then be compared with, and identified as, bit patterns of the selected character. E13B is used in the USA, where it originated, and in the UK. Another MICR font, which originated in France and is used in Europe, is CMC7. This includes the digits 0→9, the letters of the alphabet, and five special characters. The symbols are made up of seven magnetizable lines with *six spaces of varying width* between them. A wide space generates a binary 1, a narrow space a 0. We saw in chapter 2 the variations that are possible with 6-bit patterns (See Fig. 2.2). The speed of reading MICR is around 1200 documents a minute.

MICR systems employ character styles designed expressly for machine recognition and, therefore, the characters have to be accurately formed. They also require magnetic ink. These factors make for expensive printing, but one useful advantage is that characters printed with ink containing magnetizable particles can still be read even when overstamped, as may be the case with bank cheques. MICR readers cannot verify, they can only identify. With a cheque, someone still has to verify the amount to be paid, to whom it is to be paid and, most importantly, that the signature authorizing the payment is correct.

c) **Optical Character Recognition (OCR):** It is not only hand-writing which varies. Different typewriters and different typesetters produce the letters of the alphabet in a variety of forms, shapes and sizes. Nevertheless, there are certain characteristics which are peculiar to, and common to, each letter, however it is produced.

OCR readers examine each character as if it were made up of a collection of minute spots (Fig. 3.6). Once the whole character has been scanned, the pattern detected is matched against a set of patterns stored in the computer. Whichever pattern it matches, or nearly matches, is considered to be the character read. Patterns which cannot be identified cause rejection. OCR readers can read at a rate of up to 2,400 characters per second. They are generally designed to operate at slower speeds at which they are then more accurate and can handle characters which are not quite so perfectly formed.

A wide range of fonts, using ordinary inks, can now be accepted by OCR. It is possible that a computer could be programmed to accept *some* signatures, but it is unlikely that it could ever be programmed to accept every type of signature. Even so, devices have been developed which can read *neat* hand printing (capital letters rather than lower case) in black ink, and with sufficient accuracy for this to become a viable form of input.

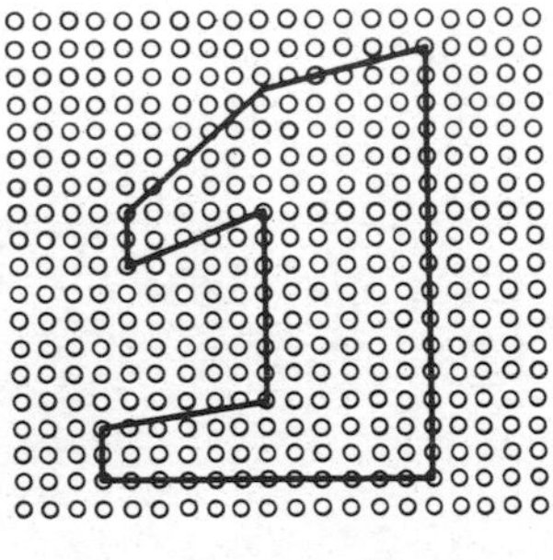

Fig. 3.6

Path 3: Teletypewriter Terminal

With all the forms of input considered so far, the data is first prepared using a separate device. However, it is possible to communicate with the computer directly by using a keyboard machine. A teletypewriter terminal, sometimes called a teleprinter terminal or a keyboard/printer terminal, usually combines a keyboard for manual input of information with a printer for outputting a 'hard copy' (printed record) of the input, system information and program results. The printing device outputs one character at a time at rates between 10 to 40 characters per second on continuous rolls of paper (typically 8 to 20 in. wide) or on 'fanfold' paper, according to the application.

Some terminals display information on a screen as opposed to printing on paper. These are known as *Visual Display Units* and are discussed later in this chapter under the general heading of 'Output' (see page 41). Many terminals also have a facility for punching and reading paper tape. This enables information to be copied and retained in coded form so that it can be used again later without the information having to be 're-typed'.

One of the features of a terminal is that it can be situated some distance from the computer. It must, therefore, include some means of transmitting information. Some terminals are designed only to send information and some only to receive, but in general both functions are carried out.

Terminals may be connected to a computer in one of two ways.

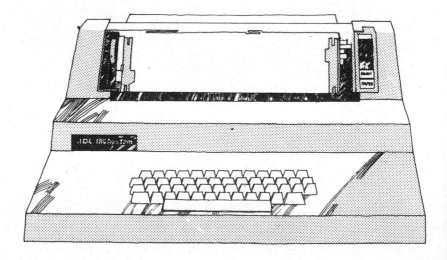

Fig. 3.7

Some are connected *locally,* by direct cables lines. This is known as 'hard-wiring' and does not usually extend more than several hundred feet from the computer itself. The second method is via a *remote* link, either by telegraph or telephone line,[3] or by micro-waves. Whilst it is probable that the 'remote' terminal would be some distance from the computer, it is possible that it may be on the same site as the computer, even in the same room. The terms 'local' and 'remote' refer to the way in which a terminal is linked to the computer rather than to distance, i.e., it is *directly* connected (hard-wired), or *indirectly* connected through other means. Both methods permit the simultaneous linking of several terminals in several locations to the one computer, with each terminal making use of the computer in turn. This is known as *time-sharing,* a concept which is developed in some detail in chapter 6.

Terminals extend the use of the computer to various places of work. They are widely used for such tasks as stock control, entering orders, updating accounts and seat reservations. The terminals found in shops and stores (point-of-sale terminals) might combine several of these tasks whilst also acting as cash registers. They can be sited at various points on a factory floor to record and receive information on different stages of an industrial process. The development of compact portable terminals has extended their usefulness still further.

Terminals now provide an extremely important and effective communication link with the computer. Their versatility, combined with the fact that they can be situated away from the computer, has led to a rapid growth in their use, and for many applications they are now the standard input device.

The reading of bar codes is a relatively new method of input and is generally associated with the use of terminals, e.g. point-of-sale terminals. A scanning device or pen reader records information from labels depicted by bar codes. The labels vary in size and in the code format used. Essentially lines or bars represent numbers or characters, with thickness and position in relation to adjacent bars distinguishing one character from another.

A pen reader is stroked across the pattern of bars and the information is captured. Codes are used to assist with inventory control, checking library books, and as labels on items in stores and supermarkets.

OUTPUT

We have seen that there are several paths by which man can communi-

---

3. A terminal linked by telephone needs a device called a *modem* to convert the information into a form in which it can be transmitted. A second modem is required to re-convert it at the other end of the telephone link before the information is input to the computer.

cate with the machine. There are, also, several ways in which the machine can communicate with man.

Printed Output

The most common method of obtaining output is via a device known as a *line printer.* Rows of character sets (fonts) are either wrapped around a drum or affixed to a chain. The drum or chain revolves across the path of a series of hammers, each of which corresponds to a print position. As the character to be printed is selected, a magnetically controlled hammer presses it onto an ink ribbon and thence onto paper, rather like a typewriter works.

A variety of stationery is used, with special designs to suit particular applications, such as pre-printed electricity bills and rate demands. Forms can also be multi-part (where copies are required for different departments), with several sheets impregnated with carbon or separated by interleaved carbon paper. In general, though, the paper used on drum and chain line printers is known as 'continuous stationery'. The paper can be plain or lined, is usually fan-folded and perforated for separation into convenient lengths (11in. typically and about 15in. wide) and comes folded in boxes, usually in ream (500) multiples.

The lines printed would normally consist of up to 120-136 characters or symbols. Different character sets are used. Sets of 48, 64 and 96 characters are typical. The 64-set has more special characters than the 48-set, and the 96-set prints in lower-case letters as well as upper-case (capitals). It is even possible to print in Hebrew and in Japanese. Line printers perform at speeds from 200 to 2,000 lines per minute. Chain printers are faster than drum printers and produce better quality output. They are, inevitably, more expensive. Line printers use an impact (letterpress) technique. In addition, there are *electrostatic* printers which form the character images by photo-chemical means. These are some two to three times faster than the conventional high speed line printers, can produce characters in both upper and lower case, and can even reproduce drawings and graphs. They are also much quieter. Despite these advantages they have limited applications because of the considerable cost of the specially treated paper which is essential to the process.

Graphical Output

Information can be output in graphical form using graph plotters. These are usually slow but the accuracy (to within 1/100 or 1/1000 of an inch) is more important than speed.[4] There are two basic types, drum and flat bed.

The drum plotter is usually restricted to one pen and can only plot onto paper. The paper is stretched over a drum. The motion of the drum, back and forth, provides vertical movement, whilst the pen, suspended from above, is driven horizontally, from side to side. The plot size is restricted in one direction by the width of the drum, which is typically up to 3ft wide, and in the other by the length of the roll of paper itself. It is used particularly for the plotting of conventional graphs and to assist with design, e.g., in textiles.

The flat bed devices, as the name suggests, plot on paper (or some other material) which rests on a flat bed. The pen moves vertically and horizontally across the bed. One directional movement is supplied by a gantry which straddles the bed and runs on rails at either side. The rails allow movement up and down the length of the bed. The other direction is supplied by a pen turret running to and fro across the gantry itself. A variety of colours, in biro or ink, can be used and some flat bed plotters can etch plastic or metal plates. The plot size is restricted by the area of the bed. Some very large beds used in aircraft design, for such things as wing profiles, can be up to 20ft by 50ft.

Visual Display Units (VDU)

A visual display device uses a cathode ray tube (CRT) to display

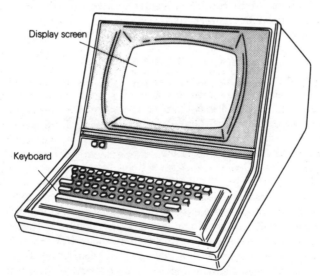

Fig. 3.8 Typical Visual Display Device (CRT)

4. The computer is unlikely to output directly in graphical form because of the considerable *mis-match* between the speed at which the CPU operates and the speed of the plotting device. The output is likely to be transferred to magnetic tape or paper tape first, and then plotted from the information on the tape.

information. It looks like a TV screen and is similar in other respects. VDUs are used particularly in situations where information is required quickly and where perhaps there is little advantage in having a permanent record of the information.

The VDU is really a type of terminal, with a keyboard for manual input of characters to the computer and with a screen for character display of output. Information is displayed very much more quickly than by the conventional keyboard/printer terminal (teletypewriter) and it is almost silent in its operation. The VDU is used, for example, in airline seat reservation where speed is the essence in handling customer enquiries and it is also used in modern computer installations to display information in the computer room for the benefit of computer operators. One disadvantage is that there is no hard copy of the output and this could be considered a limitation. However, in the type of applications for which VDUs are suited, where the display provides information on which action is taken immediately, a printed copy of the output may not be required. It is possible to add a printing device, should it be considered necessary, but this increases the cost considerably.

The most common display method is to generate characters from a 'dot matrix'. A selected pattern, typically five dots wide by seven dots high, is illuminated to form a character. A screen can usually display between 500 and 2,000 characters.

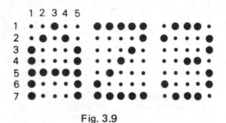

Fig. 3.9

Graphics VDU: This type of VDU is able to display graphs and diagrams as well as alphanumeric characters. It is a specialized piece of equipment, very much more expensive than the conventional VDU, and is used particularly as an aid to design. Via suitable software it can enable a design to be viewed from different angles (for example, in car and ship design and in constructional and civil engineering applications) and the design can then be modified as necessary. Graphics make considerable programming demands on the system, and these sophisticated types of display are usually linked to large, powerful computer systems, or to smaller machines which are solely used for this one purpose.

A copying device can be used in conjunction with a graphics VDU to provide hard copy of any display. A link up with a Computer Output Microfilm device (see next section) is particularly significant. It enables the recording of a whole series of graphs or designs which can then be viewed later at leisure to assist in the selection of an optimum design.

Computer Output Microfilm (COM)

A computer output microfilm device translates information held on magnetic tape into miniature images on microfilm. The device displays the information as alphanumeric characters on a CRT screen and it then records this display onto film, usually 16 or 35 mm. As each display is completed (perhaps equivalent to a page of lineprinter output), the camera can be controlled (programmed) to move onto the next frame of film.

A special reader or reader/printer can be used subsequently to view the processed film. The reader operates on a 'back projection' principle displaying a frame at a time on a translucent screen, typically about A4 size. The printer can then produce a hard copy of what is presented on the screen, probably using an electrostatic method.

Microfilm, in roll form or **microfiche,** is small and easily stored and the speed of recording is some 25–50 times faster than the average line printer. The equivalent of thousands of pages of computer output can be stored in a small drawer and the cost of the microfilm for a page of output is less than a sheet of line printer paper. Once the film has been processed it can easily be duplicated and full size hard copy prints made quickly and inexpensively.

A COM system is ideal for use in applications where there is a large amount of information to be retained which is required only for reference purposes, as with archives. Companies may need to retain records of such things as bills and invoices for a number of years before destroying them. COM provides an easy way of doing this with the retrieval of information taking only a matter of seconds using a compact desk-top viewer. COM is also ideal when multiple copies of reports or information are required.

COM systems are relatively expensive to install and are associated with big computer users. Small and medium-sized computer users who need microfilm are more likely to take their files to a bureau offering a COM processing service.

Attention has now turned to providing a mechanism to input directly from microfilm. Some CIM (Computer Input Microfilm) equipment is already on the market but it is not yet widely used.

Audio Response Unit

The computer can be used effectively to trigger verbal communication via an audio response unit and this may be an appropriate method to use if standard replies to requests for information are all that are required.

Messages are composed and transmitted in coded form to the audio response unit. The device matches the code with those of words and phrases which have been pre-recorded. The words are retrieved and a verbal reply delivered. For the sake of clarity the computer delivers the message more slowly than normal speed. Limitation on the size of the vocabulary is a hindrance to development, though within the context of a single application it may not be unduly restrictive.

BACKING STORES

We indicated earlier that a computer's memory is limited in size, is needed as a working space for the current program, and only retains information on a *temporary* basis (chapter 2, page 29). However, computers may often work on vast amounts of data and backing stores are used to retain the data on a *permanent* basis. Information stored on these devices can be retrieved and transferred speedily to the CPU when it is required.

Several different devices can provide this additional storage space, but the one selected will depend mainly on how the information needs to be accessed. There are two methods of access, *serial* and *direct*. Information on a serial device can only be considered in the same sequence in which it is stored. This would be suitable, for example, for dealing with a mailing list where each address needs to be accessed in turn. However, should an address be required out of order, it can only be retrieved by searching through all those addresses which are stored before it. Frequently, we need to access information in a more direct manner than serial devices allow. For example, at any given moment in a bank, some customer will be requesting details about his account. Backing storage devices exist which permit access to individual information in this more direct or immediate manner.[5] These direct devices are also called *random* access devices because the information is literally available at random, i.e., it is available in *any order.*

Magnetic Tape

Magnetic tape provides only serial access. It can be referenced many times without the need for replacement. In addition, information can be erased by recording new information in its place. The tape has a ferromagnetic coating on a plastic base, is usually ½in. wide and comes

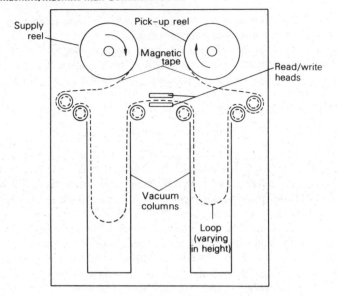

Fig. 3.10 Typical Magnetic Tape Drive

in reels of 50 to 2,400 feet. It is similar to the tape used on a tape recorder except that it is of higher quality and more durable.

Information is retained on the tape in the form of magnetized and non-magnetized spots (representing 1's and 0's) which are arranged in tracks, typically seven or nine, running the length of the tape. To represent a character in tracks, special codes are needed, just as they are for paper tape. Information recorded on magnetic tape is stored at the rate of 556, 800, 1,600 or even as dense as 6,250 characters to the inch, with the higher densities applicable to the more modern systems using nine-track tapes.

Turning to the tape drive itself, it can be seen (Fig. 3.10) that the tape runs from a supply reel to a pick-up reel via two vacuum channels and between a set of read/write heads. The two vacuum channels are designed to take up slack tape, acting as buffers to prevent the tapes from snapping or stretching when starting from a stationary position or slowing down from full speed. The read/write heads are present either to access information, or to place information on the tape. They are a single unit, made up of one read/write head per track.

Even though information can only be accessed serially, magnetic tape is very widely used. Frequently it is necessary to copy information and to retain it in the same order for use on another occasion. Tape is

5. Each item of information held on this type of store is associated with a location address, in much the same way that information is held in the main memory.

ideal for this purpose as it is cheap and the transfer rate to and from the computer's main memory is relatively fast.

Besides acting as an area of secondary storage, magnetic tape is also an input/output medium in its own right. Information is input to the computer from the tape for processing and information is output to tape where it resides until it is needed again or until it becomes redundant and is erased.

Magnetic Disk

This device has direct access.[6] In shape, a disk resembles an L.P. record. A disk pack consists of a number of these disks, six or more, mounted about half-an-inch apart on a central hub which rotates, spinning the disks at speeds of 2,000 or more revolutions a minute. Information is recorded on both sides of each disk as a series of magnetized or non-magnetized spots, i.e., similar to magnetic tapes.

Information is stored on tracks arranged in concentric circles, with each character represented by a pattern of bits in sequence on one track. Although varying in length, each track contains the same number of characters, which means that tracks on the outer reaches of the disk are less densely packed with characters than those nearer the central hub.

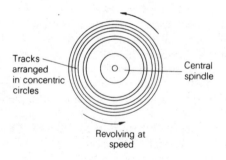

Tracks arranged in concentric circles

Central spindle

Revolving at speed

Fig. 3.11 A Disk Surface

A standard 14in. disk contains 800 tracks per disk surface, with each track capable of storing 15,360 characters. It can be seen that these are potentially very high capacity storage areas.[7]

The disk pack on some disk storage devices is permanently fixed in position, whilst on others the pack can be removed and replaced by another in a matter of seconds. The facility to change packs means that storage space can be increased without the heavy expense of buying another complete device.

There are two types of read/write head units for magnetic disk

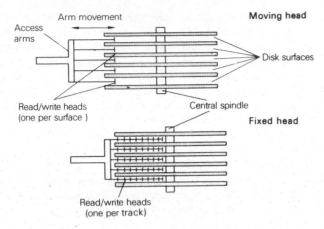

Fig. 3.12 Vertical cross-sections of read-write head units for magnetic disk packs.

devices, a moving-head unit and a fixed-head unit (see Fig. 3.12). In the moving-head unit, the head moves horizontally across the surface of the disk so that it is able to access each track individually. There is a head for each surface and all the heads move in unison. Information stored on the tracks which constitute a cylindrical shape through the disk pack are therefore accessed simultaneously, a significant factor in storage arrangements. In the case of the fixed-head unit, there is one read/write head for each track, as a result of which no head movement is needed and information is therefore traced more quickly. The heads do not have direct contact with the surface but 'rest' on a cushion of air. The air movement caused by the revolving disk forces the head to 'fly' about 1/400th of an inch from the surface.[8]

The time taken to access information on these direct, or random, devices varies considerably, but an average of 35 milliseconds is typical for a moving-head device, and 20 milliseconds for the fixed-head device. As with magnetic tape, on magnetic disk information can be accessed again and again. When fresh data is recorded it simply replaces the existing information.

Floppy Disk

The floppy disk is a comparatively new storage device. It is a small random access disk which, like all secondary storage devices, can be

6. It can also be used in serial mode if required.
7. 15,360 characters x 800 tracks x 10 surfaces per 6-disk pack (only 10 surfaces as the outer surfaces of the top and bottom disk are not used) = 122,880,000 characters per pack.
8. Dust particles can be a problem.

used both for input and output operations. Information is held on a flexible disk frequently referred to as a diskette, encased in a cartridge about 8 inches square and weighing less than 2 ounces. The cartridge is readily loaded into, and unloaded from, a drive unit. Its storage capacity is small compared with other conventional disk devices but impressive for its size. Typically, the floppy disk has about 70 tracks on which information is stored, giving a capacity of between 250,000 and 500,000 characters (equivalent to 3,000 to 6,000 fully punched cards). It is a low-cost device particularly suited to recording at the point-of-sale and supporting mini-computer systems, e.g. small business computers[9] and word processing systems.[10]

The following table summarizes the more important characteristics of the conventional backing store devices and compares them to the size and performance of the internal memory of the CPU.

Type of store	Capacity in millions of characters		Time taken to access an item of information in milliseconds (thousandths of a second)		Character Transfer Rate per second	
	Small	Large	Slow	Fast	Slow	Fast
Magnetic Tape	10–30 for a standard 2400 ft. tape		Not meaningful as the device only permits serial access to information		20,000	300,000
Magnetic Disk (movable head)*	2	300	80	20	150,000	800,000
Magnetic Disk (fixed head)	6	600	50	8	200,000	4,000,000
Internal (CPU) Memory	.016	4	1,800 Nanoseconds (thousand millionths of a second)	100	500,000	10,000,000

Fig. 3.13*The smaller capacity disks operating with moveable read/write heads may also be *removable* disk packs. The potential capacity of such a storage device can be multiplied by the number of packs available, but only one of which can be used at a time. This is also true for magnetic tape storage devices.

Input Direct to Backing Stores

In earlier computer systems punched media were the most common form of input but today the emphasis has switched to magnetic media. Keyboard devices now exist which enable information to be transferred directly to different types of backing store. Three methods are distinguishable:

    a)   Key-to-Tape
    b)   Key-to-Cassette/Cartridge
    c)   Key-to-Disk

When the information is eventually transferred from these backing stores, the backing stores themselves become 'input' devices. From keyboard to computer is yet another communication path.

a) Key-to-Tape: A key-to-tape device, sometimes referred to as a magnetic tape encoder, permits the recording of information directly on magnetic tape. An operator, copying from documents, keys the data electronically using a typewriter-like keyboard. The data is stored temporarily by the device and typically displayed on a CRT for visual checking before being transferred to magnetic tape.

b) Key-to-Cassette/Cartridge: Information can also be keyed direct to small magnetic cassette tapes or cartridges and later transferred to standard magnetic tape for processing. A cassette, typically two and a half inches by four inches in size, is capable of storing around 200,000 characters of information. A typical cartridge is smaller in capacity, averaging around 30,000 characters. These key input devices are easy to use and compact, and are therefore most suitable for the collection of data at source, for example at places remote from the computer installation.

c) Key-to-Disk: As with key-to-tape systems, information is entered via a keyboard and a copy displayed on a CRT to allow a visual check. A key-to-disk system normally comprises a minicomputer, a number of key stations and a disk drive. The minicomputer is required to control the input from the various stations, enabling the data to be held temporarily for verification and editing before allocation to the disk store.

In large office and business organizations, where traditionally data

9. See Appendix 1
10. See chapter 7.

C.C.—E

preparation is a major part of the work, keying information directly to disk or diskette is becoming standard practice. As a method it is superseding the use of the punched card.

* * *

Backing stores serve two purposes. They supplement the internal memory of the computer when linked to the CPU, and they also store programs and data for *future* use. It is important to appreciate that information from backing stores has to pass into the internal memory (under the direction of control) before it can be used (see Fig. 3.14). This means that the CPU handles information from backing stores in much the same way as it handles information passing to and from conventional input/output devices.

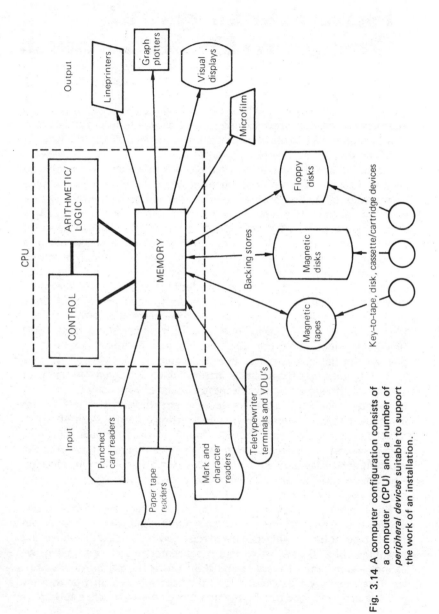

Fig. 3.14 A computer configuration consists of a computer (CPU) and a number of *peripheral devices* suitable to support the work of an installation.

4

Principles of
Flowcharting and
Program Development

The previous chapter discussed the various devices for input and output of information. We shall now extend our investigation into the ways in which we instruct the computer what to do.

We will know in general terms the problem which we are going to ask the machine to solve. Consequently, we would form an overall plan of the solution to the problem, and then reduce the solution into a series of separate (discrete) steps in some particular sequence. (This detailed solution is called an *algorithm*). To illustrate the sequence of steps in a diagrammatic form, programmers sometimes make use of a *flowchart*. However, it must be stressed that this does not mean, necessarily, that flowcharts are the best means, indeed, some computing experts refuse to use them at all, preferring instead one of the other means by which to aid the description (documentation) of their programs, for example, by the use of *tree-charts* and *decision tables*, both of which are discussed in Appendix 3[1]. We choose to describe flowcharts since they provide the simplest approach to program planning for the examples used in this chapter.

The first formal flowchart is attributed to John von Neumann in 1945, and although they have become associated with computing, there is nothing magical or profound about them. Indeed, they are similar in concept to cooking recipes and to knitting patterns, both of which show the procedure (algorithm) to follow in order to bake a cake or knit a sweater. A flowchart, then, is simply a method of assisting the programmer to lay out, in a visual, two-dimensional format, ideas on how to organize a sequence of steps or events necessary to solve a problem by a computer.

When a human being is asked to solve a problem, we assume that he or she has a certain amount of background knowledge, has certain simple facts at his/her fingertips, and has acquired certain deductive and reasoning skills. But when we ask a computer to solve a problem, we cannot assume any of these innate skills on its behalf. In other words, we have to ensure that we give it all the necessary information to carry out the problem. It is this fact which a beginner to problem solving by computers finds difficult to appreciate. In the examples which follow, this point will be brought out in more detail.

EXAMPLE 1: SEQUENCE

Problem: Dig a hole and bury a treasure chest.

List of steps to a human: 1) Pick up a spade;
                            2) dig a large enough hole;
                            3) place chest in hole;
                            4) fill in hole.

Remembering that we have to tell a computer everything, it will be seen in the following flowchart that the above four steps (sufficient for a human being) have become thirteen. The flowchart portrays the overall sequence of events by which the problem can be solved and indicates the level of detail required to instruct a computer.

We have used different shapes to mean

= Do something

= Decision (?), yes/no reply

= Stop or start

and we have linked those shapes with arrows to show the direction (flow) of events. We have included two large looping arrows which indicate that a group of events may have to be repeated; and we have put 'yes' and 'no' on the correct arrows leading out of the decision box. Remember that where a decision has to be made, the question has to be phrased so that only two answers are possible — 'yes' or 'no' ('true' or 'false') but *never* 'perhaps' or 'maybe'. According to whichever answer is valid at a given time ('the hole is not large enough yet to bury the box' or, later, 'the hole is now large enough to bury the box') the sequence of steps will change. Getting the computer to perform the correct sequence of events at the right time is what we call the *logic* of a program.

The shapes we have used above (and the others which follow) are understood and accepted by most computer people. Since there is little room in the shapes, we have to use *clear and concise English*. This factor, together with the generally understood shapes and the use of

1. Several other methods exist which are not discussed in this book, e.g. HIPO charts (an IBM development and acronym for Hierarchical-Input-Process Output), Warnier-Orr diagrams, structured programming using step-wise refinement, etc. The actual method used often depends upon personal taste or the dictates of a programming manager.

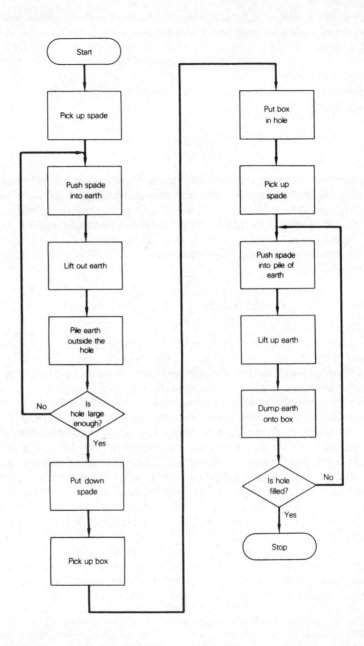

Fig. 4.1 Flowchart for Example 1

directional arrows, combine to create an overall picture of events which can be checked to ensure that no step has been left out and that it does solve the problem in hand. A senior programmer, for example, may want to check a junior's work to satisfy himself that once the program has been written, it will work correctly. This he can do by looking at the flowchart.

The flowchart normally starts at the top of a page and the yes/no arrows can leave the decision box in any direction. Try making a flow-chart to describe 'how to make a cup of coffee'. Some of the simplest tasks that we take for granted can be the hardest to describe, e.g., see if you can make a flowchart to describe 'how to tie laces (or an apron or a tie)' and see if someone else can follow your instructions without confusion. It may be more difficult than you think.

EXAMPLE 2: INFORMATION TO BE RETRIEVED

A librarian is given the title of a book and is asked to provide the following details:

1) Is the book in the library?
2) If so, what shelf should it be on?
3) What is the author's name?

The librarian may already know these facts from experience, but if she does not, then she will have to find out. In a manual system, this will mean going through a card index file (by title) and reading each card until the one is found which contains the title, as well as the shelf number and the author's name. If the title is not found, then the librarian knows that the book is not in the library.

In a computerized system, all the librarian would have to do is to type in the title of the book at a teletypewriter device and let the computer perform the search using a pre-stored program. If the computer finds the title in its pre-stored library catalogue, then it will print out the required details, perhaps on to a visual display unit; otherwise, if the title is not found, then it will print a message to the effect that the book is not in the library. Figure 4.2 illustrates a flowchart for the search part of the program. We assume that the search program has already been brought into play and that the computer system has a list of all books kept in the library. This flowchart introduces another accepted symbol to represent an input or output instruction, viz.

An efficient information retrieval system could do much more than merely provide the shelf number and the author's name. By making a reference to a list of all books currently on loan, it could, amongst other things, also indicate whether the book is currently on loan and, if so, to whom and the due date of return. Chapter 7 discusses further information retrieval applications.

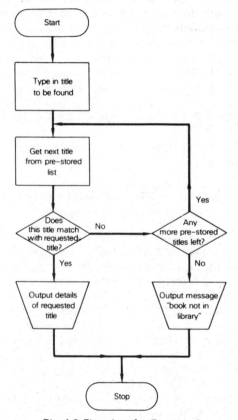

Fig. 4.2 Flowchart for Example 2

EXAMPLE 3: COUNTING – POPULATION SURVEY

Let us suppose that a population survey has been carried out in a given district, and that the information received from the survey has been transcribed onto punched cards. Since the cards have 80 columns each, one card could contain such data as the name, address, sex, age, profession, etc., of each person surveyed, in much the same way that we saw in chapter 3 (page 33).

The problem we shall solve in flowchart form is quite simple, but it does illustrate how to count and select only certain relevant data from a given block of associated data. Our problem is to find the number of adults (aged 18 years or more) in the district under survey. The computer will be told to 'look at' each data card in turn and if the 'age' is equal to or greater than eighteen, then '1' will be added to the adult count. Otherwise, the computer will ignore that card and be told to read the next one. In Figure 4.3 we see how our problem might be represented by a flowchart.

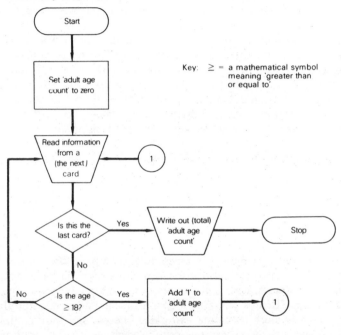

Fig. 4.3 Flowchart for Example 3

There are three points to note. First, the adult count must be set to zero at the start of the program. This is something that a human being would do automatically (and without thinking) in a manual system. Secondly, the programmer must instruct the computer to read another card if the current age is found to be less than eighteen. Again, a human being would not have to be told this if the exercise were performed manually. Thirdly, there is a problem when the last item of data has been read. A human being would know that he or she had read the last data card. But a computer does not know. For all it 'knows' there may still be another card. In other words, the programmer has to inform the computer in some way that there are no more cards to look at. There are several ways of doing this. Our flowchart illustrates one method. An *additional* card is inserted at the end of the data cards containing a special piece of information. It indicates that the last data card has been read. Only when this information has been encountered will the computer move on to write out 'the total number of adults'. There may be many hundreds of data cards to scan and the necessity to check each one to see if it is not the last one may appear extravagant, but this is computing!

These three points highlight how programmers need to approach the solution of problems by computer. It is this unusually fundamental approach which is often difficult to grasp when one starts to learn programming.

Another shape is introduced which is called a 'connector symbol'. A flowchart for a complex problem could well cover several pages. If there is insufficient space on a page for the next shape, or if too many lines would confuse the chart, then an arrow is drawn into a connector symbol (Fig. 4.4) containing a unique number. A reader now looks for another connector symbol with the same number, but with an arrow pointing into some other shape, and continues from there.

Fig. 4.4

A completed flowchart is *not* a complete computer program. It is an aid to programming. It defines the procedure and the logic involved. From our examples, we are in a better position to understand what this 'logic' means. There is only one shape, the rhomboid or decision shape, which permits more than one exit-path. The decision box contains a question and, depending on the answer at any given time, only one of two directions may be taken. For example, to repeat a group of steps, as we saw when the hole was not large enough to bury the chest, or to continue when the hole was large enough.

A flowchart may seem simple to prepare, but you will find that much practice is needed in order to think through a problem in discrete, logical steps, to assume nothing and to forget nothing. Not everyone will tackle a problem in exactly the same way and, in consequence, several different flowcharts could be drafted, or, indeed, some other form of diagrammatic representation be used for the same problem. When presented with a problem, we usually have a few rough ideas on how to solve it. These are jotted down and examined more closely. Then another idea occurs and the first draft is altered. Before long our flowchart begins to look like Spaghetti Junction, lines may go off in all directions, over and under other lines which have been crossed out. But this is normal. It is from the rough drafts that the final flowchart is produced. But this is not the end of the affair. Before a problem can be successfully handed over to a computer for solution, there are at least three stages[2] involved before the problem can be input to the computer. First, the algorithm has to be thought out. This is then represented in some diagrammatic form. Finally, and only after the programmer is sure that the logic is correct, comes the *coding* stage, when the flowchart is reworded into a programming language. This latter exercise is relatively straightforward. All the hard work goes into the production of an accurate flowchart. In the next chapter, we shall examine the various levels of programming languages and consider in more detail what is involved in the coding stage.

2. See page 70 for a more complete list.

5

Computer Languages

With our natural, or native, language (English) we can communicate to one another our ideas and emotions. Natural languages are highly developed and with them we can express not only facts but also abstract ideas, and we can convey shades of meaning or suggest subtle feelings and sensations. But in order to do so, a large vocabulary is required.

With a computer 'language', the programmer communicates with the computer which, being a machine, is receptive only to simple, unambiguous facts. A programming language, therefore, uses a limited or restricted vocabulary. Indeed, a programming language by its very nature and purpose does not *need* to say very much. We have seen in chapter 4 that a problem has to be broken down into discrete (simple and separate), logical (sequential) steps. We also saw, in chapter 1, that the apparent 'versatility' of the computer is based on the fact that all of the many different problems which can be solved by computer are reducible to an interplay between four fundamental operations — input and output operations, arithmetical operations, movement of information within the CPU, and logical or comparison operations. We shall return to this point later in this chapter but for the moment we simply want to establish that a programming language merely needs to reflect these four basic machine operations.

People can use natural languages *incorrectly* and still make themselves understood. Computers, however, are not yet able to correct and deduce meaning from incorrect instructions. Computer languages are smaller and simpler than natural languages but they have to be used with great precision. Unless a programmer adheres *exactly* to the 'grammar' of a programming language, even down to the correct 'punctuation', his commands will not be understood by the computer.

It should be appreciated that a given machine is designed to react to or obey only one language or code. If it is presented with a program written in another language, then that program will have to be translated into the language which the machine has been designed to accept.

Since the inception of computers, three types of computer language have evolved;

a) Machine Codes;
b) Assembly Codes;
c) High-Level Languages.

We shall now examine the evolution and nature of each type of language.

Machine Codes

To understand the structure of a machine code, there are two facts discussed in chapter two which we need to recall. The first, is that a machine instruction has a two-part format, viz.

OPERATION (Code)	ADDRESS (Location)

Fig. 5.1

The second point is that both parts are represented internally in the machine's store as a string of binary digits. It should be no surprise, therefore, that some of the first programmers (those, for example, who worked on the Manchester Mark 1[1]) actually wrote their instructions in binary. However, since human programmers are more familiar with the decimal system, most of them preferred to write the two-part instructions in decimal, and leave the input device to convert these into binary. The set of instruction codes (whether in binary or decimal) created in conjunction with the computer designer, is called a *machine code* or *machine language*. It will be determined by the actual design or construction of the ALU, the control unit and the size, as well as the word length,[2] of the memory unit. Clearly, because of the dependence of the language on the particular machine, such languages are called machine-dependent languages.

Assembly Codes

The *numeric* machine codes (decimal or binary) are often difficult to remember and, even with a code book or glossary, encoding is a laborious process and mistakes can easily be made. This led to the use of *mnemonics* (or memory aids) which the human brain can more readily identify. A computer may be designed to interpret the machine code of 1001 (binary) or 09 (decimal) as the operation 'multiply', but it is easier for a human being to remember it as MULT or MLT.

1. See Appendix 1.
2. Matters become more complicated here because some computers have *variable* word lengths and others have *no* word length but merely a succession of bit places.

A repertoire of codes evolved, therefore, using readily identifiable mnemonics, e.g., DIV (divide), SUB (subtract), etc. Easier though this made life for the programmer, it made things more involved for the computer.

The MLT has to be translated into the binary pattern '1001' before the machine can 'understand' the operation intended. The act of translating is carried out by a special pre-stored program called an *assembler*. It translates the program written by the programmer into that version which the machine recognizes and responds to, and 'assembles' it in the main memory ready for execution, hence the term *assembly codes.*

Machine and assembly codes, being orientated towards the basic design of computers, are referred to as 'low-level' languages.

High-Level Languages

The commercial viability and wider use of computers led, by the mid-1950's, to the necessity for, and development of, 'high-level' languages.

These languages, instead of being machine based, are orientated more towards the problem to be solved. Such problem-orientated languages enable the programmer to write instructions using certain English words and conventional mathematical notations, therefore making it easier for him to think about his problem. This means that the two-part format of a low-level instruction (operation code/location address) is no longer necessary in a high-level instruction. As an example, we give a high-level instruction (in FORTRAN — See appendix 2) to 'multiply two numbers together and add a third number to their sum'. The familiar algebraic notation for this is: $x = a \times b + c$.

FORTRAN, being orientated towards the solution of mathematical problems, allows the programmer a similar ease in describing the same instruction, thus: X = A * B + C.

The only differences between the two forms are FORTRAN'S use of capital letters and an asterisk in place of our more familiar multiplication symbol.

Compilation Process: By using a high-level language, the programmer saves himself a great deal of time and effort. To describe the above mathematical expression in a low-level language the programmer would have to write perhaps five instructions instead of one.

The computer, of course, cannot directly understand a high-level language. A translation stage is necessary. Assembly languages use an assembler to perform this conversion process. High-level languages use instead a *compiler* (a more complicated pre-stored program) to translate the programmer's instructions (the source program) into its machine-level counterpart (the object program) which the particular machine has been constructed to obey. Note that the source program and the object program are the *same* program, but at different stages of development.

The FORTRAN compiler is only capable of translating source programs which have been written in FORTRAN and, therefore, each machine will require a compiler for each high-level language which is used. Furthermore, it should also be appreciated that each machine will have to have its own 'personal' compiler because an object program for machine X will not be the same as the object program for machine Z.

Compilers are large programs which reside *permanently* on secondary storage. When required they are *copied* into the main memory.[3] The processes of compilation *and* execution take place as one, followed-through operation. The compiler, being a program, is executed in the CPU. Its data is the source program statements, or instructions, each of which is converted into the appropriate machine instructions in binary, and then stored in the main memory of the CPU as the object program. The compiler, having performed its work, is no longer required. The space it has taken up during compilation (the translating process) is then used by the object program for manipulation of the data, the results of which can then be output.

We have considered the three types of programming languages. In most cases, programmers mainly work in a high-level language, but low-level languages are still used by those programmers who need to work at machine level.[4] There are many high-level languages, but they can be grouped into four broad application areas; scientific, business, special purpose and interactive (see appendix 2). The language chosen will be largely determined by two factors: the first being the application in hand and, the second, the choice offered by the computer installation, i.e., the range of compilers which are available.

A SHORT PROGRAM

In this section, we shall attempt to present at concept level what programming is like, what is involved from the machine's point of view, and how the computer solution is reduced to reflect the four basic operations of a machine. The approach we have taken is of necessity a relatively simple one. In practice there are a few more complications. But since this is not a programming text, many questions will have to remain unanswered. Those who wish to pursue the subject in more depth should refer to the Bibliography for further reading.

3. The next chapter discusses in more detail how the computer is 'told' in which language the source program is written.
4. See chapter 10.

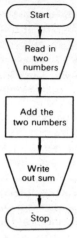

Fig. 5.2

a) Simple Problem

Our problem is to 'write' a program to read two numbers off a data card, add the numbers together and write out their sum on a line printer. The flowchart for this is illustrated in Fig. 5.2.

b) High-Level Version

The high-level language which we shall use is a pseudo one, it does not exist, but is similar to many which do. The program will consist of five statements (instructions) in our language.

Statement	Meaning
1) BEGIN	Inform the computer where the program begins.
2) READ B,C	Read two numbers (from a card), associating the first with location B and the second with location C.
3) X = B + C	Add the numbers stored in locations B and C, place their sum in location X.
4) WRITE X	Output the contents of location X (to the line printer).

5) END Inform the computer (control unit) that the end of the program has been reached.

This is a short and simple program for illustration purposes only. If someone wanted to know the sum of two particular numbers, it would be quicker to add them up himself. But programs are seldom written for any one set of data. Usually, they are written to handle any data which could be related to the problem so that the program can be used again and again with only the data changing each time. In other words, they are a method or algorithm. This can be achieved, as we have done in the above program, by using the general formula (X = B + C) instead of the actual numbers to be added up on a given occasion.

When you recall that the letters refer to the *address* of a location and not its *contents,* then this procedure makes more sense.

It is normal when using high-level languages to use mnemonics for addresses in store rather than actual numbered locations. The letters B, C and X (any other letters could have been chosen) refer to three locations in the memory of the CPU. The high-level programmer never knows exactly where his program and his data areas will be in main memory. Consequently, he *cannot* give precise numbered locations in his program instructions. It is part of the duty of the *operating systems* software[5] to give the mnemonic addresses actual (physical) numbered locations. *How* this is done will not concern us in this book.

We know that a high-level language cannot be understood by the computer and that a translating (compiling) process has to take place. Our five high-level statements will have to undergo compilation so that they can be reduced to machine-level instructions. Fig. 5.3 shows our

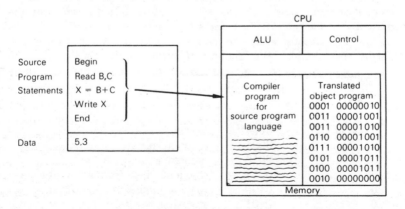

Fig. 5.3 Compiling the program

5. See chapter 6.

source program followed by the two data numbers (in this instance 5 and 3). A copy of the compiler for our pseudo language has already been brought into memory and is ready to compile the source program.

After our source program statements have been translated, the space occupied by the copy of the compiler is then used as a working area by the object program for the manipulation of data.

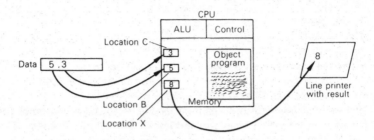

Fig. 5.4 Execution of Object Program

c) Machine-Level Version

We indicated that high-level language statements free the programmer from having to phrase his instructions in the formal two-part instruction format necessary with machine codes. But let us see how, when the source program has been compiled, the resultant object program, which does use the two-part instruction (operation code/location address), might then appear. Using a twelve-bit word length (for illustration purposes), we shall allow 4 bits to represent the operation code and 8 bits for the address portion. Our code is hypothetical because we are not concerned with the design features of a particular machine. We choose, therefore, quite arbitrarily, the following numbers to represent certain operation codes, i.e., those which will handle input/output, internal movement of data within the CPU, and arithmetic.

Decimal	Binary	Meaning
01	0001	program starts
02	0010	program ends
03	0011	read a number (from an input device)
04	0100	write a number (to an output device)
05	0101	store number *from* the accumulator
06	0110	load a number *into* the accumulator
07	0111	add
08	1000	subtract

09	1001	multiply
10	1010	divide

.
.
.

Using these ten codes, our five high-level statements will appear in a machine acceptable program (the object program), as follows:

Step	Op. Code	Location address	Meaning
1	0001	00000010	Begin program (code 01) at location 2
2	0011	00001001	Read a number (code 03) into location 9
3	0011	00001010	Read a number (code 03) into location 10
4	0110	00001001	Load into accumulator (code 06) the contents of location 9
5	0111	00001010	Add (code 07) to value in accumulator, contents of location 10
6	0101	00001011	Store (move) value from accumulator (code 05) into location 11
7	0100	00001011	Write out (code 04) the contents of location 11
8	0010	00000000	Program ends (code 02)
.			
.			
.			

Fig. 5.5 Object Program

The four bits for the operation allows up to 16 possible codes, whereas the address portion allows up to 256 separate address locations.[6] In the following figure (5.6) we will assume that our operating system (see chapter 6) will place the binary object program in locations 1 through to 8, and locations 9 to 11 will be used as a working area for data manipulation.

If we examine the machine instructions, we see that our high-level source program of five statements has increased to eight. Since there are two numbers to be read, there will be two machine instructions at the machine level, one for each number.[7] In the high-level version only one was necessary. But the most interesting expansion for our present purpose is that the statement "X = B + C" has been re-coded into *three* machine instructions (steps 4, 5 and 6). Once the two numbers have

6. We are not implying that *all* 12-bit word length machines have only 256 locations. Techniques exist which can increase an 8-bit address to refer to over 4000 locations, that is a 4K store.

7. In practice, inputting numbers from any input device is more complicated. But the high-level programmer need not be concerned with the problems.

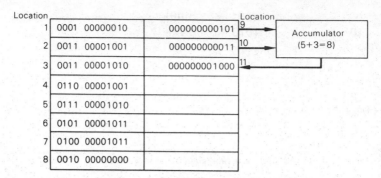

Fig. 5.6 Object Program in Main Store

been stored in separate locations (the purpose of the input operations), they have to be added together in the arithmetic unit by means of the accumulator register (see chapter 2).

The programmer does not need to know anything about the accumulator other than that it performs the arithmetic which he has commanded. Although in the original statement locations B and C and X were used, the machine has to equate these 'names' with actual addresses, and this is something which the operating system itself will do. In our example, locations B, C and X have been given the numbered locations of 9, 10 and 11 respectively. The first number is moved into the accumulator by the machine instruction, 0110 00001001, i.e., operation code 06 with the address of location 9. Next, the add instruction (07) has the address of location 10. This instruction now adds the contents of location 10 to whatever value is already contained in the accumulator, i.e., the contents of location 9. Having successfully added our two numbers, instruction 05 then moves the result of the addition from the accumulator to location 11 (location X referred to in the source program).

Note how these three machine instructions can be expressed concisely in one high-level language statement.

* * *

Logical/Comparison Operations

We have looked at the solution to the simple problem at various levels, from its flowchart stage, to the coding into a high-level language and, finally, to how the instructions are broken down by the compiler so that they can be understood at machine level. This example brought into play three of the basic operations which a computer can handle (input/output operations, arithmetic operations, and internal movement of data). It is the fourth, the logical and comparison operation which allows interesting things to be done via programs, because this facility enables instructions to be repeated and treated differently according to the current situation. The looping forward (or backwards) to repeat one or more instructions has been shown in the flowcharting exercises. Without this feature very few useful programs could be written. It is a simple technique but one upon which computing hinges. A basic set of machine codes would therefore need to include some such instructions.

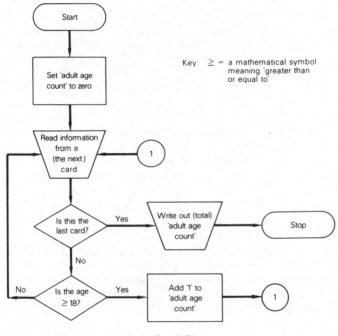

Fig. 5.7

Taking the flowchart of the population survey in chapter 4, let us write the high-level statements to represent 'if the age is greater than or equal to 18, then go on to that instruction which adds one to the adult age count; if it is less than 18, then go back and read the next card.' In our pseudo language all this can be said less verbosely, thus:

IF (AGE *less than* 18) THEN JUMP TO "read next card"
                  OTHERWISE "add '1' to adult age count"

This one statement will be broken down into three machine code instructions. Using our basic set, and a loop (jump) instruction which we shall give the code 11, our object code will look like this (in decimal for ease of reading):

06 — 043   the current AGE (read into location 43) is loaded into accumulator.

08 — 044   subtract 18 (stored at an earlier stage in the program in location 44) from the value in the accumulator.

11 — 020   *after* subtraction, if the result in the accumulator is negative (i.e., AGE is less than 18), then jump to "read next card" (we have assumed that the machine has this instruction (03-043) stored in location 20). It will then read the next age.

If the result is *not* negative (positive or zero, i.e., the age is greater than or equal to 18), then go on to the next step in sequence, "add '1' to adult age count".

Note that if the age 21 had been read off the survey card, the result of subtracting 18 would be 3, i.e., a positive number; if the age had been 17, the result would be — 1, i.e., a negative number; if the age had been 18, then the result would be 0. Therefore, by subtracting 18, we obtain either a positive, or a negative or a zero result. We can now appreciate the purpose of '11' as a machine instruction. It makes the machine test for a negative result. If this is so, then the program 'knows' that the age tested was not an adult age and, consequently, goes back to read the next card. Thus, three jump instructions are needed in a basic set — jump if negative (the one we chose because of the particular circumstances), jump if positive, and jump if zero. Our basic set would include these instructions numbered, say, 11, 12 and 13 respectively. It is possible with these thirteen basic machine commands to perform any combination of the four fundamental operations of a computer.

Development of a Computer Program

Before a programmer can begin his task, he will require two specifications. The first will detail the precise problem to be solved, and the type of information which is required. The second will itemize the computer configuration which will handle the job, i.e., the available equipment. We now summarize the seven stages with which a programmer is concerned in the development of a program, from the specification of the problem to its successful completion.

1) **Algorithm:** The construction of the algorithm (method of solution) is the stage which requires creative thinking. The programmer may first set out the algorithm in broad terms to help visualize possible alternatives.

2) **Flowchart:** The next step is to record the algorithm in a flowchart

form. By using suitable data the programmer can then check the validity of his logic.

3) **Code into a High-Level Language:** The sequence of operations outlined by the flowchart is transposed into a programming language. Preprinted coding forms are normally used in this exercise.

4) **Input Preparation:** The instructions must now be prepared in some form suitable for the computer to receive them, i.e., punched cards, paper tape, or directly input at a teletypewriter.

5) **Compilation:** The source program is fed into the computer and the compiler converts it into a machine version. At the same time, the compiler scans the source program for any *syntactical* errors, i.e., grammatical mistakes in the use of the language. Messages, known as *diagnostics,* pinpoint the grammatical mistakes and are printed out for the programmer's attention.

6) **Corrections:** Syntax errors are corrected, and the source program goes through the compilation process again. Only when the program is syntactically correct, is the object version passed on for execution.

7) **Testing Process:** The compiler can only detect errors in the *syntax* and not in the *logic* of the program. It is the programmer's task to create instructions which are logically sound and in the correct sequence. Any faulty logic that still remains can only be detected by examining the output. When testing, specimen data of the type the program has been designed to handle will be fed in, including deliberate errors to make certain that the program is capable of identifying them. If it cannot distinguish between valid and invalid data, the programmer will have to go back to step 1 to rethink his algorithm.

* * *

Programmers are usually concerned with a general problem rather than a particular problem, i.e., add *any* two numbers together rather than two *specific* numbers. For example, when asked to program a firm's payroll accounting system the program must work, not only this week or this month, but every week and every month that it is used. In some cases, programmers may be asked to solve a particular problem when it is a very large one, e.g., to monitor the moon landing or to prepare an index of the works of Thomas Aquinas, but such a program must still work for every likely eventuality that may arise during solution of the problem, however short its life may be.

Programs now exist to solve many diverse problems. When the

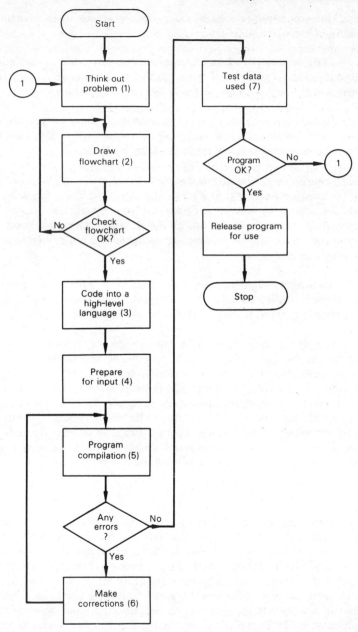

Fig. 5.8

general, or potential, computer user needs a particular task to be done, his programmer, whether a member of staff or the external representative of a manufacturer, may well be aware of existing programs which could be modified to fit. For example, the program for firm A's payroll system could be adapted to fit firm B's needs. In many cases, however, modification of a program can be more complicated than the creation of a totally new program. Because of this, *adaptable* programs capable of more general use have now been evolved. They are known as *packages*.[8] Nevertheless, whether using a package or a totally new program, the programmer still has to check, re-check and check again to insure that the program does what it should and that it will continue to do so for as long as it is required.

8. See also chapter 7.

6

Introduction to Computer and Operating Systems

One might well believe from popular statements such as:
"I wrote a program for a computer"
"All our accounts are now processed by a computer"
that computer users come face to face with computers. But this is far from the truth. Few people today communicate *directly* with a computer. Instead, they communicate with a computer *system* (via an *operating system*). But, there are several types of computer systems — batch processing (which was first developed in the 1950's), multi-programming, time-sharing, and real-time systems (which have evolved since the mid-1960's). What are these systems and how do they vary?

In this chapter, we shall briefly examine these systems, roughly in the order of their historical development. It is hoped that what will be remembered will be *why* such varied systems exist, since it is not possible here to describe in any detail *how* they work. We hope that the material presented will encourage you to pursue the subject further. There are abundant articles and books upon the subject, a few of which are listed in the Bibliography.

Early Computer Configurations

In the early days of computing, if one had a problem for computer solution one first had to build a computer. SEAC is an example of a machine especially built for the particular needs of the National Bureau of Standards. The designers of such computers, or their close associates, also programmed the solution and, in many cases, performed all the necessary duties which an operator would perform today (feeding cards to the card reader, paper to the line printer, manipulating switches, etc). They had an intimate knowledge of their machine and could follow the progress of a program via the pattern of lights displayed on the control panel(s), known as the *console,* which showed the instruction currently being executed, the addresses involved, the contents of registers (the accumulator, for example), and so forth. When the program was completed, the programmer left the machine free for the next person. The configuration (hardware) then in use was simple, as

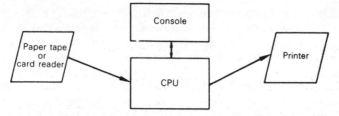

Fig. 6.1 A Simple Configuration

Fig. 6.1 suggests. There was an input device (card reader or paper tape reader), the central processing unit, an output device (usually, a line printer), and a console which allowed instructions to be directly keyed into the CPU, and which also displayed the calculations or data manipulations which were taking place inside the CPU.

Programmers today do not have the same intimacy with their machines as their predecessors. The change in relationship has come about because of the increasing differences which soon evolved between the awesome speeds of processors and the relatively slow peripheral devices. Formerly, internal processor speeds were much slower and there was little appreciable disparity between the speeds of the input-output devices and the central processor. What difference did exist was tolerable in the circumstances. It may appear a small enough issue but it is the essence of *why* computer systems evolved.

Peripheral and CPU Speeds

Let us examine more closely the difference in speeds between the CPU and its peripheral devices.

Card readers are able to read punched cards at speeds of between 100 and 2000 cards per minute. Taking the example of an 80-column card, this means that between 133 and 2666 characters can be read in one second.

$$100 \times 80 \times \frac{1}{60} = \text{approx. 133 chs/sec (for a 100 cpm reader).}$$

Line printers have speeds of between 200 and 2000 lines per minute. If the line length is 132 characters then they can print at rates of between 440 and 4400 characters per second.

$$2000 \times 132 \times \frac{1}{60} = \text{approx. 4400 chs/sec (for a 2000 lpm printer).}$$

Seeing the faster I/O devices at work can be an impressive experience. However, central processing speeds are even more impressive. For example, a medium large computer such as the CDC CYBER 174 can transfer internally 10 million characters per second. What does this mean in practice? If the fastest card reader is attached to a CDC CYBER 174, then in the time it takes the card reader to read one character, the computer could have handled approximately 3750. In other words, while the card reader is supplying just one character to the main store, the CPU can perform many other operations before it needs to become involved with the next character which the card reader can supply. It should be clear that if the CPU has nothing to do while waiting for the characters to be input by the reader, it spends the vast majority of its time idling. This discrepancy in speed (1:3750) is called, in computer terminology, 'speed mis-match'.

Improved I/O Performance

It will be seen throughout this chapter that it is the I/O operations which slow down the overall computing process. This situation was not so acute with the early, slower computers. But as the internal processing speeds increased, as well as the number of programs to be processed, the method whereby one programmer loaded his own cards and operated the machine himself could only lead to serious mis-use of computing power. What was the central processor doing whilst the programmer was putting his cards in the reader and running around pressing switches? The answer, of course, is that it was doing nothing. This situation was even more exacerbated when assembly languages were introduced for, then, the programmer had not only to load the cards for the program and data, but also the cards for the assembler program.[1] While the card reader was passing all this information through to the main memory, the processor was working only at the speed of the reader and not at its full potential. Clearly, some means of accelerating the I/O phases was required.

The first significant attempt came with the development of magnetic tape. Now cards could first be read via the card reader, and the information copied onto a magnetic tape. From this tape, information could then be passed to the processor at speeds between 20,000 and 300,000 characters per second. Likewise, results produced during processing could be transferred at this faster rate to a tape which, in turn, could then be output via the line printer. System programs, such as assemblers, could also be kept on magnetic tape instead of having to be read via the card reader each time they were used. The stage was now set for the introduction of *batch processing*.

Batch Processing

With the increase in the number of programs to be run, it made more sense to collect several at a time (a batch), and read them onto the input tape to form, in effect, a queue of programs. As the central processor completed one program, there was another waiting on the input tape. This method was called 'batch processing'.

Many installations extended this practice and the IBM 7094 system, once in use at Imperial College, was an excellent example of batch processing. This system involved the use of three computers, as Fig. 6.2 illustrates. The card reader was linked to an IBM 1401 computer which read a batch of cards onto a magnetic tape. This tape was then rewound to become the input tape for the main processor (the 7094). Results were fed from the processor to an output tape. When the entire batch had been processed, the output tape was connected to an IBM 1460 computer to transfer the program results to the line printer.

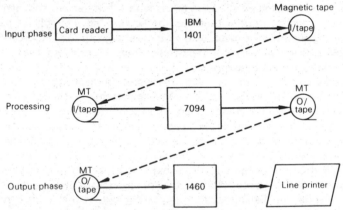

Fig. 6.2 The Imperial College (London) Batch-Processing System (1966-1971)

In this way, the main processor, the 7094, was not held up by the slower speeds of the card reader or line printer but worked at the full speed of the magnetic tapes. This process, in which the card reader and the line printer were not directly connected to the main processor, is known as *off-line spooling*. However, the card reader was 'on-line' (directly connected) to the 1401, and the line printer on-line to the 1460. The 1401 and the 1460 were called *satellite* computers and were, in effect, 'slave machines' for the 7094.

Since each phase (input, output and processing) could proceed independently, individual batches could be overlapped, thereby making more efficient use of the system. While the 1460 was printing the output for batch one, the 7094 was processing a second batch, and the 1401 was reading a third batch.

1. Before the advent of magnetic tape, it was necessary to 'load' the assembler program into main memory via a card or paper-tape reader.

Batch processing was a vast improvement over single-job-submission. In the case of the 7094 system, overlapping batches increased the number of programs which could be processed by 60%. This was due to the fact that the CPU could concentrate on *computation,* namely, arithmetic and logical operations, and the transferring of information internally within the CPU. When the CPU is unable to do any computation because it is waiting for I/O, its potential speed is wasted.

Operating Systems

An important feature which we need to consider is the *operating system.* As the name suggests, it has something to do with the work of an operator. The operator is responsible for loading and operating the card reader; setting up the tape drives with input, output and language translator tapes; insuring that the line printer has a supply of paper; recording the number of programs run; and logging the resources used (machine time, paper, etc.). The computer can be programmed to assist with some of these functions.

The secret lies in the use of certain system control commands which can be easily recognized by the operating system. In a batch or multi-programming environment which uses punched cards as the input medium, the operating system can recognize those cards containing system commands by placing a particular symbol in a certain column (such as the '£' sign in column one). By placing these 'system control command cards' at the beginning and end of a 'job',[2] one complete program (including the data for that program) can be separated from the next in the batch. If the first card includes the user's account number, the system can also log the computer time for the job. Other command cards can be used to identify the language translator required by the program. Figure 6.3 illustrates the concept.

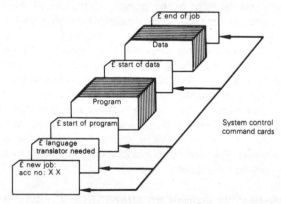

Fig. 6.3 Concept of Using System Control Commands

As each new job card (the first system control card) is encountered, it is a simple programming matter for a system program to add one to a total number of programs run and to record the computer resources used by each program. The operating system, therefore, is able to provide statistical information which is essential to management for planning the efficient running of the installation.

Today, operating systems do much more. But first, we need to look at the following computer systems so that we can then see how their increased sophistication has, in turn, made the operating system more complicated.

Multi-Programming

With batch-processing, programs are called in sequence one at a time into the central memory for processing. When there is only one program in main memory, two of the CPU's most significant features may be under-utilized, its expensive memory and the full capabilities of the ALU. Not every program will be large enough to fill central memory. Not every program will be purely computational. The large commercial type of program normally reads in vast amounts of data, performs very little computation and outputs large amounts of information. We call these programs *I/O bound,* since the majority of work they perform is input-output.

The answer is to use a multi-programming system which enables more than one program to reside in central memory at the same time, so that when program A is reading in data or outputting results (I/O operations), program B's instructions can then be executed (performed). If both programs are involved in I/O activity, then program C can be executed. The actual number of programs allowed in store at any given time will vary depending upon the operating system in use at a particular installation. Those jobs awaiting entry into the central memory are formed into a queue on a fast secondary storage device such as a magnetic disk.

For multi-programming to work satisfactorily, large memories are required (of the order of 128K), together with fast secondary storage devices and fast ALU's. Only the computer itself is capable of switching the CPU from one program to another fast enough. Hence, this task must be incorporated into the overall operating system which then becomes more complex. It will, for example, have to know:

1) when program A is performing I/O, and switch execution to program B;

2. The use of the term 'job' here refers to a deck of cards which include system control commands, program instructions and data.

2) when both A and B are engaged in I/O, and execute C;
3) when either A, B or C (whichever is first) has completed its work, so that program D can be moved from the entry queue into the vacated memory space.

That part of the operating system which performs the above functions is called a *supervisor*.[3] Its main duty is to monitor the activity of the program currently being executed, so that at the appropriate time it can switch control to another program, and control the flow of programs into the main memory from the entry queue. It must also keep all the results for the various programs in separate areas. This is achieved by allotting each program a separate space on magnetic disk (forming, in effect, a results queue ready for output). If you think back to the discussion on serial and direct access methods, it should be clear that a direct access storage device is needed for this results queue. The use of serial magnetic tape would not be a good way of achieving this. (It is possible, but the tapes would have to be continually re-wound, thus reducing the efficiency of this method.)

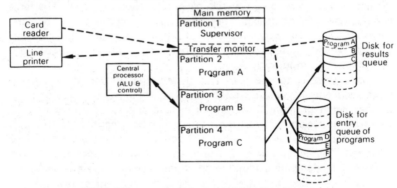

Fig. 6.4 Memory Partitioning in Multi-Programming

Fig. 6.4 illustrates the principle of a multi-programming system. The main memory is divided into sections or *partitions*. The first partition is reserved for the supervisor, which has to remain in main memory all the time. The other three partitions (in this instance) each hold a program, A, B and C. Although there are more than two programs in main memory, only *one* is ever being executed at any point in time. Program B is currently being executed and program C is passing some results to disk. Program A has completed its work and is being replaced by program D from the entry queue. Note that a second disk is illustrated to hold the results of each program in separate areas.

A part of the supervisor partition is reserved permanently to organize the transfer of these queued results from the disk to the line printer. This we shall call a *transfer monitor*. It is also used to build up the entry queue on disk, which has been input from a card reader (Program F in diagram).

When a job is submitted for processing, some time will elapse before the output is available. The length of time involved, called the *turn-around time*, will depend upon the number and size of jobs ahead of you. For some applications time is critical. Results may be needed in seconds rather than in hours. Time-sharing systems make this possible.

Time-Sharing

Users of a time-sharing system communicate with their computer via a teletypewriter device or a visual display terminal which is connected to the computer by land or telephone lines. In this way, they have a direct means of communicating with the central processor. Time-sharing systems have many, even hundreds, of terminals linked up to the central processor at the same time. However, if time-sharing is to be effective each user will require a response to a query from the computer within two to five seconds. We shall now explore that aspect of such systems which allows many users to be given this fast response.

The strategy of a time-sharing supervisor (resident in main memory all the time) is different from that of a multi-programming supervisor. The CPU can still only execute one program at a time and, clearly, the concept of one, possibly lengthy, program being completed before another one can be allowed into main memory from the input queue cannot apply here, otherwise certain users are going to have to wait for more than a few seconds before they can execute their programs. The basic idea behind time-sharing systems is to allow *all* programs to have a *brief* share of the central processor in turn. The time-sharing supervisor gives each job a short period of time during which it is in sole control of the processor. This short period of time is known as a *time slice, time slot* or *quantum,* typically 10 milliseconds.

If there are, let us say, ten terminals in use, user 1 is allowed to have his program executed and when his time period expires, or if his program becomes involved in an input-output request (thereby not requiring the central processor), the supervisor schedules the processor for user 2. User 1's program is swapped out of memory and user 3 swapped in. During this time, user 2 has control of the central processor. This swapping process, sometimes known as *roll-in roll-out,* is repeated many times within a few seconds. Thus, when a user's job is being executed it is in main store, but when it is not being executed it will be on secondary storage. Disks and drums are the only feasible secondary storage devices since they have a much faster rate of information transfer than magnetic tape and provide direct access.

3. Each manufacturer has adopted its own terminology for the 'supervisor'. For example, IBM call it the 'monitor' and ICL the 'executive'.

When it is realized that a computer such as the CDC 6600 can perform 3 million calculations in one second, and that experienced terminal users can only input information at up to 10 characters per second, and are often engaged in comparatively long thinking spells, then it can be appreciated that modern time-sharing systems can service many terminals in the space of one second.

In time-sharing systems, a transfer monitor is required to co-ordinate the flow of information between the terminals and the disk storage. It is resident in the central memory and works in conjunction with the time-sharing supervisor which is responsible for the overall operation of the time-sharing system. Fig. 6.5 illustrates these concepts and shows terminal 1's program being swapped out, terminal N's program being swapped in, whilst terminal 2's program is currently being executed.

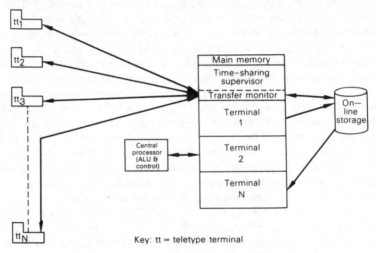

Fig. 6.5 Concept of a Time-Sharing System

Real-Time

The expression 'real-time' is applied to any system which produces an almost immediate response as a result of inputting data. The essential feature is that the input data must be processed quickly enough *so that further action can then be promptly taken on the results.*

Two examples of systems which operate in real-time are process control systems (as in nuclear reactor plants and steel mills) and transaction systems (such as airline reservations).

In a process control situation, one set of results may be used as essential data for the next stage of the process. The time interval between processing one set of data, and providing the results for the next input phase, may be as little as a few microseconds. Whatever the time interval, it is important that it is not exceeded.

In the case of transaction systems, the period may be extended to a few seconds or even minutes, rather than microseconds. But a point to note is that once a particular transaction has been processed (reserving for Mr X a seat on the 9.30 a.m. flight from Heathrow to Rome), the files need to be updated before the next transaction can be processed. Real-time systems cannot break down without causing some disruption. This is one difference between real-time and time-sharing; the latter *should* not fail, but if it does the outcome is never disastrous. In many instances, real-time systems are duplicated so that, in the event of a break down, back-up facilities are immediately available. This makes some systems very expensive but, in the environments to which they are applied, a fail-safe system is essential.

Computer Networks

A logical extension of time-sharing systems enables users to have access to more than one computer installation in order to share some computer facility or stored information peculiar to one centre. This linking together of distinct installations is called a *computer network system.* Figure 6.6 illustrates the concept in which there are four computer centres, each capable of supporting its own local time-sharing /batch users, but at the same time permitting a user to have access to any one of the other three installations in the network.

The University of London has a large network system currently involving four computer installations. Via a terminal connected to the

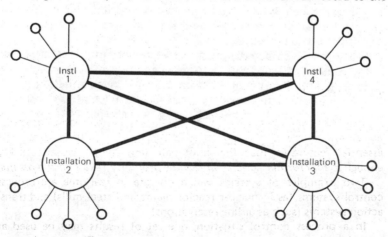

Fig. 6.6 Computer Network System. Small circles represent user terminals and/or batch card reader/line printers.

local installation, a user can access his own or any of the three other centres, so that specialized information or some computing facility (e.g. computer output microfilm) unique to one centre may be used from that user's own locality. To allow the large volumes of data to flow from one site to another, high speed (wide band) data communications are necessary which are not only fast but also reliable.

Currently, most network systems are essentially private affairs linking up large organizations with some common interest (such as banks, universities) but before long a public network system could exist in the United Kingdom and based upon a branch of the Post Office, probably by the latter half of the 1980's.

Distributed Processing

One of the most controversial areas of computer development today is *distributed processing.* It is not easy to give a satisfactory and commonly accepted definition since too many varying ones abound. However, it is generally agreed that one of the main ambitions of a distributed processing system is to place computing power where it is needed, at the computer user's own locality. Historically, and mainly for reasons of economics, individual organizations possess large centralized systems usually located at the head office. Regional offices wishing to make use of the central computer do so on a time-sharing, multiprogramming basis.

However, a centralized system has limitations; first, if the main computer fails to function (not uncommon) then all regional offices have to suspend computer operations, resulting in an inevitable bottleneck once the main system is functioning again; secondly, regional users have to format their own data at the direction of some central and often distant data processing manager.

Today, there is an increasing desire to get away from these limitations. The possibility of doing this has been due in no small measure to the growing use of low cost mini and micro systems[4] being installed at local sites. Each local centre can now process on site much of its day-to-day work and thus have direct control over its own equipment as well as its own data formats, and, if necessary, possess hardware which exactly suits its own particular requirements. (Local control will not, of course, eliminate all problems.) But this is merely a de-centralized system. To have a distributed processing system it is necessary for all the local centres to be linked together so that should one site have a computing task which the local centre cannot process by itself, then that centre can 'call upon' additional assistance from one or more of the other sites. Thus the main characteristic of a distributed system is one in which a user's task, on a given occasion, can be divided up and distributed across a number of computer installations.

Currently, most distributed systems involve the distribution of *processing power* only. Many problems still exist for the more important aspect of *distributed data files* between several computers. Consequently, it is upon this area that future development must be concentrated before distributed processing becomes the commonplace that many experts forecast.

*   *   *

Distributed processing is inevitably confused with network systems and it is appropriate to distinguish between the two. In a network system, it is *normal* to transmit tasks to other centres possessing some unique facility or stored information which the user cannot obtain at his local point of activity. On the other hand, a user in a distributed system should confidently expect that *most* of his work can be dealt with adequately by his own installation; indeed, his own site is specifically designed to perform the majority of tasks. It is only in the *exceptional* circumstances that he needs to rely on the transmission of his task to the other sites. Thus, it is possible to conceive a major banking concern arranging its own inter-organizational computing system on a distributed processing system and yet for that system to form part or one node of an inter-banking computer network system.

SUMMARY

In this chapter we have indicated that the average computer user does not usually deal directly with a computer, but with a computer system, via an operating system. Our contact with a computer complex may be through a small computer, a VDU or teletypewriter terminal. However, the CPU at the heart of the installation is surrounded by layers of software. We must not lose sight of the fact that no matter how complex an operating system may appear, all that is happening at the heart of the machine is the interplay between the four basic operations of input-output, arithmetic, logical and comparison operations, and internal movement of information within the CPU. It may be that the program is simple, adding two numbers and outputting the result; it may be the final sales statistics which lead to a mammoth take-over bid; it may be the calculation of the strength of a heart beat whereby the means of saving a patient's life can be determined. To the basic machine, none of this matters. It performs its four operations 'mindlessly', untouched by the effect of the results. But it is the intricate web of software surrounding the basic machine which makes it possible for the program to provide the great variety of information which *is* of human importance.

4. For a description of microprocessors see appendix 1.

7
Computer Applications

The computer is used to assist man in business organizations, in research and in many other walks of life. In this chapter we shall examine some of these areas so as to give an indication of the very wide range of activities in which the computer is involved. Some may be surprising, if you consider the limited capabilities of the machine. However, versatility has been provided by man's ability to reduce what are often highly complicated problems to the simple level at which the computer can be used, and to design and implement ingenious computer systems which can provide a myriad interplay of the basically simple tasks that the computer can handle.

You should remember that what has been achieved so far has been accomplished in a very short period of time. The first computer was developed as little as thirty five years ago and ten years passed before the industry was established on a firm footing.

SCIENTIFIC RESEARCH

We have seen that the first computing projects were undertaken in university laboratories and scientific institutions to develop computers for special purposes. In science, the advent of computers has meant that calculations which were previously beyond contemplation, because of the time-span and drudgery involved in carrying them out, have now become possible. This has greatly accelerated and expanded research in such sciences as physics, chemistry, astronomy and genetics. More recently there has been an increasing use of computers for research and data analysis in less mathematical areas such as medicine, the social sciences and even the humanities.[1]

Computers are now a standard feature of life in universities and industrial laboratories. Almost every branch of science and engineering has benefited from their development. Elementary particle physics is one field of study which has been broadened considerably. Molecular biology is another, resulting in spectacular progress in our understanding of the structure of living matter.

Because of the immensity of some of the research problems, huge computer complexes are sometimes needed. The CERN Institute in Geneva, researching in high energy nuclear physics, is one such centre. It is financed by a number of European governments, and has become an international pool of scientific brainpower.

BUSINESS APPLICATIONS

The first non-scientific use of computers concerned routine clerical work. Office administration had previously used such aids as punched-card accounting machines and adding machines. It was a natural progression to make use of computers. Computing procedures for clerical duties were relatively simple to develop since they were already well defined and the repetitive nature of many of the tasks made them very suitable for the computer.

Computer applications to business and commerce date from the middle of the 1950's, a decade of vigorous recovery from World War II which led to economic expansion and rapid technological development throughout the industrialized world. Today, most large and medium sized companies are very dependent on their computers for various administrative functions, whilst many smaller concerns make use of the services of computer bureaux. As we pointed out earlier, commercial data processing now accounts for some 80% of all computer usage.

Tomorrow, the impact is likely to be even greater. The cheapness of microtechnology brings computing within the grasp of even the smallest business. At a general office level, word-processing systems are beginning to influence office practice and organization. In its simplest form a word processing device consists of a 'typewriter' with storage capacity, e.g. floppy disk or cartridge disk, and a built-in package to facilitate editing, formatting and printing of text. Systems may include special purpose keyboards and printers, display features, and special purpose packages for specific applications such as producing a range of documents for insurance quotations and purchase orders.

Payroll and Personnel Records

Payroll accounting was the first commercial area to become widely computerized. The calculation of wages or salaries involves a number of variable but common factors which relate to the personal details of each employee, such as gross pay or rate for the job, tax code, national insurance, etc.

These facts are retained on backing store together with information which accumulates each time the payroll is run, such as pay-to-date, and tax deducted for the year. Hours worked, overtime and any other

1. Applications include concordances, textual criticism and stylistic analysis.

information relating to the pay package being processed forms the input data for the particular run. The program contains formulae for calculating all the deductions to arrive at net pay. It will also build up records of tax-to-date, pay-to-date, etc. It computes these details, prepares a wages slip for the employee (and, perhaps, a copy for the firm's pay office records) and writes up-dated information on the backing store for future use before moving on to consider the next employee. All this is integrated into one payroll system which may be made up of a number of related programs. They are not programs necessarily involving lengthy or complicated calculations but they save a considerable amount of repetitive manual effort.

If pay is made in cash, a program can include an analysis to calculate the exact number of notes and coins of each denomination required for the total pay out and for each individual wage packet. Another program might print out cheques to the individual bank account of each employee. Files[2] generated by payroll are frequently enlarged to include such additional information as length of service, qualifications, training, attendance, sickness and vacation records, thus providing comprehensive personnel records.

The overall payroll system with attendant personnel details and records may comprise tens or even several hundreds of different though related programs. Collectively they form a package or a number of packages. A package may be a standard software development for a particular range of computers to be produced entirely within the business concern. Increasing use is being made of standard packages. Remember, computers essentially process information and it is only information (or data) which has to be provided for a package to operate successfully. A package is designed to accept information according to a specified format and the general aim is that it should be readily usable by non-programming personnel.

The expense of a computer and the attendant system is unlikely to be justified for payroll and personnel records alone. The firm would probably use the computer (its own or one shared through a bureau) for further analyses based on the payroll program, e.g., the relationship of total wage costs (weekly, monthly, etc.) to jobs in hand, total costs to date, individual job costing, etc. This kind of information, if quickly available and up-to-date, makes it easier for management to improve its efficiency by promptly pin-pointing areas of weakness and strength.

Stock Control and Sales

Stock control, the processing of sales orders and sales accounting, sales analysis, market research, forecasting and subsequent production planning are additional areas in which the computer assists in business and commercial organizations. In all these cases the company can benefit from the immediate availability of information which the computer provides.

For example, it may be a misuse of capital to hold more stock than is needed, but customers soon become dissatisfied if delays occur because of a shortage of stock. Automated inventory or stock control, as often practised in supermarkets, provides exact information at all times so that neither of these situations should occur through ignorance of the level of stock. It would be customary for each item in the inventory to be assigned a pre-determined minimum level. (This will take into account the rate of sale and the time needed for re-ordering). When this figure is reached, the computer program outputs the information so that action can be taken.

When handling sales orders by computer, the present volume of sales is known and this information, together with past records and perhaps statistics obtained from market research, forms some of the data needed for sales forecasting, which in turn influences stock control. Basic information for billing (including discounts, shipping/postage costs, VAT, etc.) is obtained from sales orders and the computer can be used to maintain customer accounts and to print invoices. All these various applications make effective use of the machine's abilities to store large quantities of information and to retrieve items at speed, and they rely on program inventiveness to insure that information is updated promptly, accurately and usefully.

The computer is also being used more and more in everyday cash transactions. The intrusion on the public is largely unobtrusive. The cash register in supermarkets, stores and offices where goods and services are sold is no longer the traditional device it once was. Though looking similar apart from more graceful lines, it is probably a computer terminal, sometimes referred to as a point-of-sale terminal, linked to a central computer, recording information about sales as well as providing exact change for the customer.

Banking

Banking has now become almost totally dependent on the computer. In the past, a large but manageable amount of book-keeping was handled manually, but such has been the expansion in banking that a huge labour force would be needed to tackle today's massive volume of book-keeping. The computer is necessary because there is no other way of dealing with the problem. In most instances, the computer is sited centrally. Branches are equipped with terminals, giving them an on-line accounting facility and enabling them to interrogate the central system for information on such things as current balances, deposits, overdrafts,

2. For a definition of files see chapter 8.

interest charges, shares and trustee records. Under computer control, customer statements are prepared and printed out onto specially designed stationery. Cheques are handled by computers at the clearing banks, a mammoth operation normally carried out during the night when the system can concentrate on (be dedicated to) this purpose. The cheques are sorted into branch, and then customer order and returned to the branches the next day. The computer also provides each branch, and its customers, with prompt access to information from a much wider financial world than would be possible under a manual, local system.

Leading international banks and financial institutions are able to obtain up-to-date news on foreign currency rates from the world's money markets using an on-line world-wide **information retrieval** service. London, New York, Zurich, Frankfurt and Hong Kong are the major sites in the network with each city servicing its own and neighbouring countries. Data is entered and received using visual display terminals, and the processed data is held on disk storage at the central sites.

Insurance and Stockbroking

Insurance companies, finance houses and stockbroking firms also make use of computers. Here conditions and requirements are similar to those in banking. Large files of information have to be retained and updated, interest rates and bonuses have to be calculated, policy statements and renewal notices have to be prepared and payments made. In the buying and selling of stocks and shares various calculations have to be made, contract notes drawn up and files consulted and amended.

The computer is also beginning to be used as an aid to more efficient investment management. Up-to-date and accurate information can be obtained quickly by consulting data bases[3] relating, for example, to UK or foreign securities, or to the share price index. Armed with this information, the stockbroker is in a better position to use his judgement and to take decisions.

An Aid to Management

We have seen that the computer is able to provide useful information. Let us consider what this means to people in managerial positions whose task is essentially to translate   information into action. The immediate benefit is that the information provided is comprehensive and up-to-date. This means that decisions taken can be more reliable, and they can often be made in advance of a crisis rather than after it has occurred. The computer can also be used as a management tool to assist in solving business problems. In *operational* (or *operations*) *research,* which is the name given to the application of scientific procedures to decision-making, certain techniques are used which require the calculating and storage abilities which the computer can provide. **Critical Path Analysis** and **Linear Programming** are two methods of analysis which are used. These are applied in situations where a good deal of information is known concerning a number of variable factors, and where the task is to arrive at a solution which indicates the best possible relationship between the variables, taking into account whatever constraints there are. The **Simulation** method is used where decisions have to be made on the basis of probability and where some of the information used in the analysis is itself predicted, and where past events have to be taken into consideration before arriving at a decision. In assisting in the decision-making process the computer *uses* rather than provides information.

INDUSTRIAL APPLICATIONS

In industry, production may be planned, co-ordinated and controlled with the aid of a computer. The computer may also be used to direct the operation of individual machine tools (drills, lathes, saws, etc.) and even to operate assembly machines which piece together parts of equipment (e.g. electrical and mechanical appliances, sections of motor cars and even complete vehicles). The use of numerically controlled machine tools directed by computer-produced tapes can speed up production, ensure greater precision and reduce scrap wastage. In certain industries (chemical, oil refining) the computer can be used to monitor and regulate total processes without human intervention, just as it can to control air conditioning and heating systems in modern multi-storey buildings.

The control of a chemical plant by computer can be a much safer and more efficient method than by manual control, since changes in conditions which occur during a process can be detected and compensated for immediately. It would, however, be normal for human operators to maintain surveillance over the total process so as to be able to intervene should the need arise.

Oil refining, the separation of crude oil into its many component oils, is a continuous process and it depends on the maintenance of certain conditions throughout the process. These two factors make refining a suitable application for computer control. Instruments measure such variables as temperature, flow and pressure. Any deviation from the standard is detected and regulating devices are adjusted to bring the process back into line.

3. A collection of information relating to a particular subject. A large data base is generally referred to as a data bank. The effectiveness of any data base of information depends to a great extent upon the efficiency and convenience of the means of access to the information in store.

Electricity

Starting up a power station involves many complex operations which have to follow a strict sequence with set time limits between each operation. This is a laborious, time-consuming task but one for which the computer is well suited. The computer is also used by electricity authorities for load control. Demand for electricity is not constant throughout the day nor throughout the year. Generators have to be phased in and out to meet changing situations. Because of the time lag required to build up the necessary power, fluctuations in the load have to be anticipated in advance.

Under computer control, past records stored in the system, relating to changing hourly demands under various weather conditions, are scanned and compared with the actual, present loads in different parts of the supply network. Predictions are then made and generators are set to start and stop at certain times. This insures that extra power is transferred to those areas where it is most needed at peak periods. It also insures that those generators which have to be expensively fuelled with precious natural resources (oil, gas, coal) are not run wastefully when the demand for power drops.

Steel

Process control applied to certain parts of steel production has increased efficiency in the industry. One example is in the cutting of the steel into lengths to match the firm's order book. In the rolling mills, which run at great speed, red-hot steel billets are rolled out into strips. The billet size is not known accurately to begin with and, as each is rolled out, the length increases until the required thickness of sheet or diameter of rod is reached. Before the use of computers, the mill would cut the sheets or rods, of varying lengths, into standard sizes or a particular size for one order. The lengths of steel left over would be scrap which would have to be resmelted, resulting in a lower grade steel. With the advent of computers the amount of scrap was reduced to a minimum, for it became possible to calculate the lengths that the billets would make whilst still red hot and being rolled out. This information could be matched against a table of orders for the type and quality of steel being rolled, in time for the flying shears (computer controlled) to cut the strips in the best way.

Printing and Paper

Computers are used by the printing trade where they are particularly useful in the production of newspapers and magazines where strict deadlines have to be met and time is short. Articles can be transposed to magnetic (or paper) tape and then rapidly typeset, under computer control, in several type sizes, widths, and depths as necessary. Complete texts may be retained on tape, enabling amendments to be incorporated easily when reprinting. Computers are also used to update the listings in telephone directories, catalogues, parts and price lists so that they can be quickly typeset whenever required.

In the manufacture of paper there are continuous processes, predetermined standards have to be maintained, and wastage has to be minimized. Computers assist the paper mills with process control in ways similar to those described in the chemical, oil refining and steel industries.

Engineering Design

The design of any piece of engineering, whether an airplane, ship, car, bridge, road, building or machine, should not merely be pleasing to look at. The piece of engineering must not only be able to perform the tasks intended for it over its economic or anticipated life, but it must also be able to withstand all foreseeable mishaps during its working life. Engineering designs, however sound they may seem to be on paper, have to be physically tested under simulated or real-life circumstances before becoming operational.

Computers can help in calculating that all parts of a proposed design are satisfactory. If modifications are necessary and further calculations are required, the computer can evaluate the alternatives more quickly and more accurately than would otherwise be possible. This means a great saving in time and elimination of technical faults and human error (which could possibly be disastrous), before a design is further developed.

Computers can also be used in calculations of space and layout as well as strength requirements. This not only helps insure that engine parts are accessible for maintenance, and bridges and tunnels high and wide enough for unusual traffic; it also insures that there is enough room for everything — passengers, fuel, cargo, etc. On motorway construction, the computer can calculate the amount of soil needed to raise an embankment, or the amount of rock to be removed in cutting through a hill, and it can work out the most efficient movement of such materials.

When fitting the structural and spatial requirements of an engineering project into an overall design, the computer can also help with graphical output. The facility to view a design from all angles while it is still on the drawing board, and then to be able to modify it quickly, avoids having to spend time and money building and testing several designs before determining which is the right one. The computer can provide graphical and perspective views to show the shape of a proposed aircraft wing or car body, the slope of a curve for a new road, the visibility that the pilot or motorist will have, or the accessibility of the instruments that he might have to operate.

Computers are also used as an aid to electronic circuit design, even assisting engineers in designing circuits for other computers.

METEOROLOGY

Predicting the weather has long been considered something of a mystique based on country signs and folk lore. Meteorology, as a science, is relatively new and, with computer assistance, it has become more of an exact science. The problem in meteorology has always been to obtain sufficient data, and to analyze that data quickly enough so that predictions can be made. Satellites, linked directly with computer systems, now provide the meteorologist with information, in addition to the data obtained from weather stations on land and at sea. Armed with more information, the relationship between the variable factors which constitute weather can be analyzed in greater depth, and a more accurate prediction of future behaviour can then be made. The computer system is also able to analyze vast quantities of past measurements to test for weather patterns and, based partly on these results, long-range forecasts can be made. Many of the people who depend upon reliable, up-to-the-minute weather forecasts (those concerned with air travel, shipping routes, storm rescue operations, farmers, etc.) do not always realize the extent to which they have become dependent upon computers.

SPACE TECHNOLOGY

The development of space technology which culminated in the first moon landing was only possible because of the calculating powers and speed of the computer. Computers were used at the design stage of the project and in all phases of development right through to flight control. For example, they monitored and helped to control the proper functioning of all the equipment; they helped determine the routes (trajectory paths) and kept surveillance during the flight; they plotted courses of action when unforeseen events occurred; and, finally, they processed information relayed from the space vehicles.

The last point is significant because the collection of information is the main reason for putting satellites into orbit. Computer-linked space satellites provide previously unavailable information about the universe around us. This information is not merely of interest in scientific research (such as astronomy), but it increases our knowledge of our own planet (in geology and mineralogy), and it is of immediate practical value, for example, in meteorology. Satellites are also used as long-range beacons or micro-wave reflectors to provide the immediate world-wide coverage of important events by TV and radio that we now take for granted, but which was inconceivable even a generation ago. The computer has played a leading role in, and continues to be an integral part of, these new wonders of the second half of the twentieth century.

COMMUNICATIONS

Air Travel

Air traffic control, which is responsible for organizing the safe movement of our crowded airlines, depends on a significant amount of computer support. As flying speeds increase, control decisions have to be taken more quickly.

This also applies to the pilot who has to react not only to instructions relayed to him from traffic control, but also to changing situations during flight (variations in atmospheric pressure, wind speed and direction). Various instruments, dials and meters indicate the state of the flight and the current weather conditions. These provide the pilot and the flight engineer with the information they need to control the flight and to make navigational calculations. It takes time, however, to scan the instruments and to assimilate the information, and time can be critically precious at the speed at which the plane is flying. Small computers, made possible by the development of compact integrated circuits, can be installed as part of the plane's equipment. These computers are programmed to continuously analyze data, which is relayed direct from the various instruments, and to provide co-ordinated information to the pilot in time for human decision and action. Control itself can also be invested in the computer so that, when certain conditions arise, automatic corrective action is immediately taken without the need for slower, human intervention.

Besides the many in-flight uses, the computer plays an increasingly vital role in the training of pilots. A flight simulator provides an exact replica of the flight deck and performance of an aircraft, enabling the equivalent of many hours of flying to be undertaken without leaving the ground. The computer resolves the tasks, monitors and controls the pilot's action, and maintains a record of the pilot's performance.

At ground level, the information needs of a busy airline are extensive. Computers are used for the efficient handling of seat reservations, crew schedules, timetables, tariffs, cargoes, maintenance schedules, personnel records, accounting, and stock control. Large scale air travel has developed quickly in recent years and computers have helped to make it a very reliable, and safe, form of transport.

Computer controlled seat reservation brings benefit to customers and to the airlines. It is an economic necessity that airlines operate as near to capacity as possible. To avoid over-booking, a complete list of all bookings needs to be maintained and be available for immediate interrogation. This is achieved by using communication networks, covering whole continents, which link the booking offices to a large computer system working in real-time. Communication between continents is established by using transoceanic cables and satellites. A travel agent is able to find out the current status of any flight and can book seats on the basis of the information obtained. This is all done in a matter of seconds and, when a seat is reserved, the information system is automatically up-dated.

Computer controlled seat reservation is also applicable to hotel rooms, theatre seats, and bookings for sporting events at large stadiums.

Transportation

Other transport facilities are making increasing use of computers. Railways prepare timetables, scheduling at the same time the distribution of the rolling stock to operate their services, and they control busy stretches of track with computer assistance. Computer controlled ticket machines to facilitate the automatic checking of tickets are likely to be introduced on busy main line stations and by London Transport on the Underground system. Shipping companies devise the best method of loading and storing cargo, using computer programs which are designed to take into account such variable factors as size, weight, solidity (the ability to stack in layers), destination and urgency. The computer in conjunction with radar and other monitoring equipment can also be used to make increasingly crowded shipping lanes safer, e.g. the English Channel. Haulage firms and transport concerns may determine optimum routing. If, for example, a vehicle has twenty delivery points, a computer program can consider all the various route options and pinpoint the shortest or the best route if other variable factors (such as avoiding travelling empty, combining several deliveries, refuelling) have to be taken into account.

Traffic Control

Maintaining the flow of automobile traffic in congested areas is of paramount importance and an ever-increasing problem. The computer already assists with the control of traffic lights in some of the world's major cities, and many more conurbations will probably adopt this method of control. A single computer-based traffic system controls an area of nearly 200 sq. km. in Tokyo and the system is being expanded year by year. Results are impressive if not always apparent to the motorist. Individual sets of traffic lights normally change after a set period of time, regardless of the volume of traffic. A network under computer control operates instead on the basis of the volume and flow pattern of the traffic at the time. Information regarding the volume, detected by measuring devices on approaches to all sets of lights as the traffic moves, is transmitted to the computer system. This information, representing a total overall view of the distribution of traffic, is related to permanently stored information regarding distances between lights and the permitted traffic speeds. As a result, the various lights over the whole network are changed to maintain maximum flow. Some systems can even trigger warning signs advising drivers of the optimum speed at which they can maintain continuous movement.

It is not unusual for television cameras to be installed at major traffic junctions so that potential trouble spots can be kept under surveillance. With pictures displayed from various vantage points, and a reporting system which indicates when a particular set of traffic lights has broken down, human operators can watch over the network and intervene when the occasion demands, promptly directing police and repair crews to the exact spot(s) where they are required.

LOCAL AUTHORITIES AND PUBLIC UTILITIES

Local authorities, central government departments, and state controlled public utilities all have to maintain extensive records. Indeed, in a socially conscious, heavily populated, industrialized environment, the tasks of officialdom today are of such a scale as to be impossible without computer assistance. The State is the biggest collector and collator of information, and the usefulness of the computer in storing, retrieving and analyzing information is greatly increasing the scale on which it is collected. Computerization is also encouraging the centralization of information for greater convenience and accessibility in large data banks.

The computer is used extensively to carry out routine clerical functions, supplementing rather than replacing clerical staff, undertaking, for example, the preparation and printing of rate and tax demands, gas, electricity and telephone bills. One national centre is responsible for maintaining all driving licence records and for issuing renewal notices and licences. Similarly the registration of vehicles is handled by computers in regional centres. The computer is also playing an increasingly prominent part in the organization and running of the public health and social services, in the maintenance of law and order, and as an aid to education.

Telephones

Computerized telephone exchanges handle an ever-increasing volume of calls. They do so more quickly and with less likelihood of error than would otherwise be possible, and they can be linked up to other networks/exchanges for wider, prompt use. Cross-country, and even overseas, calls which previously meant a slow link-up through several switchboards and/or operators, can now be made directly and quickly. The computer can also maintain a log of calls for subsequent billing.

Medicine

The uses of the computer in the medical field are partly analogous to applications in business and industry. We find, for example, the computer being increasingly used in hospital administration for such tasks as maintaining inventories of drugs, surgical equipment, and linen; for payroll; hospital accounting; and for bed allocation. Information on the condition of patients, details of tests and clinical reports may be stored on a computer system. This combined information can be used to provide ward and patient summary reports and, where a terminal has been installed for the use of the ward nursing staff, the system can provide instructions and reminders concerning the care of individual patients.

In intensive care units the computer can be used to monitor a patient's condition. Scanning instruments attached to the patient are linked on-line to the system so that nursing staff can be notified as the patient's condition changes. The computer may print out or display a log of the patient's condition, drawing attention to measurements that fall outside the critical limits set by the doctor, or the computer itself may trigger directly the necessary corrective action.

In some clinics the computer is used, albeit in an experimental way, to "interview" patients before or after they see a doctor in order to collect information for the patient's records and even to assist with the diagnostic process. It is suggested that patients are more relaxed, and honest and frank with their replies when faced with an impersonal machine.

The computer may assist in medical diagnosis, for example programs exist which can carry out electro-cardiagram analysis to determine both normal and abnormal heart conditions. The computer system can act as a vast encyclopaedia of medical knowledge, providing the doctor with access to an ever-increasing quantity of information which he could not possibly hope to carry in his head. Diagnosis itself is a complex process, and the symptoms of a disease are not consistent in all patients. The consultant makes a diagnosis on the basis of information he has gleaned from the patient's condition. He can then carry out a dialogue with the computer system, testing his hypotheses (perhaps referencing other recorded cases) until he is satisfied that his diagnosis is correct. The computer can help, but the experience of the consultant remains all important.

The computer may assist in prescribing the correct dosage and pattern of treatment, for example, in treating cancer by radiotherapy where it is vital that the correct dosage of radium is administered and only to the exact area required. Computers are being used to make these delicate calculations. Using data provided by the consultant, the computer produces a treatment timetable complete with the calculated dosage for the individual patient.

The computer has an important part to play in medical research and in the teaching of doctors and nursing staff. The ability that a computer system has to retain information on a large scale means that detailed records of case histories of particular illnesses can be available for scrutiny in sufficient quantities to assist medical research. 'Models' can be constructed in the computer system to simulate the behaviour of various parts of the body, for example, the lungs and the heart. It is also possible to use computer programs to test the effect that a form of treatment might have on a patient before it is administered.

These different medical applications are in various stages of development. Some of the ideas we have discussed are not yet in widespread use, but enough has been achieved to indicate that the potential benefit of the computer, to both patients and to an understaffed medical profession, is considerable.

Law and Order

The enforcement of law and order depends to an extent on the availability of up-to-date information. Police forces make extensive use of the information retrieval capability of computer systems for this purpose. Records are maintained concerning accidents, vehicle owners, disqualified drivers, traffic tickets, stolen vehicles, fingerprints, criminals, wanted and missing persons, stolen property and drugs. Some of these records are stored on microfiche. It is important for police in all regions to have access to these files of information and for response time to enquiries to be immediate; crime is not local and it does not stand still. A large network of terminals is needed with each terminal linked on-line to a large central computer system. Networks can be linked together, e.g., through Interpol, for fast, world-wide investigation of cases of international significance.

Libraries and Museums

Increasing use is now being made of computers in library organization. Lists of borrowed books are maintained by the system and reminders for those which are overdue can be generated by computer output. A tally of the number of times books are taken out can be kept. More significant is the number of various ways that the contents of the library may be referenced with computer assistance for the benefit of users. Not only can all the books be classified by subject matter but, by page and paragraph references, information relating to particular topics within the subject can be pin-pointed. This has particular implications for legal and technical libraries where detailed references frequently have to be made and cross-references are of considerable value. Some university libraries in North America are linked to a network so that an obscure document in a distant archive can be quickly located and, in some cases, photocopies can then be telexed over a wide area.

Museums are also making use of computers to help with cataloging and indexing. Information about the exhibits in a museum's collection is assembled and retained as a large data base, and the information retrieval capability of the computer can then be exploited to the benefit of staff and visitors. Some museums are linked in a communications network to allow the exchange of information between different computerized museum data bases.

Education

The learning process can be enriched in many subjects because of the scale and range of information which a computer data bank can provide. Use is now beginning to be made of the computer as a resource in teaching and learning at all levels of education.

Instructional material can be prepared and stored within the computer system in the form of programs which are carefully structured to teach specific lessons. A student could then sit at a teletypewriter terminal or VDU and call in the program and participate in the lesson. This form of teaching aid has been used successfully to supplement more formal teaching methods. The program can be used by many students, thus freeing the teacher to spend time on more personal tuition.

The computer can also be used to *manage* the learning process. Programs can be designed to test for particular skills and knowledge, and then to direct the student to the next learning phase depending on the individual's results. This may mean a step forward or several steps back to repeat a previous lesson. The managed system also records all results and provides up-to-date information for the teacher on each student's progress.

Computer programs can be designed to create 'models' for experimental purposes (e.g., simulation of experiments in physics) which a student can use, discovering for himself what happens in given situations. The computer provides the opportunity for experiments to be carried out which would not be feasible in real life, because of dangers, costs, etc. The computer can also be used time and time again with different sets of data so that a variety of conditions can be studied.

Students, particularly in higher education and those studying science and technology, also benefit from being able to use the computer as a computational tool. They learn a programming language and write programs to solve some of their course work problems, treating the computer as an aid in much the same way as a slide rule or a set of mathematical tables.

The computer can relieve the teacher of some administrative duties, giving him more time to concentrate on teaching. For example, the computer can be used to assist in constructing timetables; to monitor and schedule teaching resources; to build up and maintain comprehensive student records, to provide a complete student profile; and to accumulate information, internal and external, for assistance in careers guidance.

* * *

Computers were evolved partly to meet the needs of war. They have been developed for peaceful purposes and have helped to bring the world closer together, to expand it, and to offer visions of other worlds which were previously unattainable.

The first computers were designed for a few specialized uses. Technological development has extended the range of uses, and today's computers encompass a wide spectrum of applications — warlike and peaceful, particular and general.

But knowledge brings responsibilities as well as benefits, and the social implications of the computer are discussed in chapter 11. Here, we have been concerned merely to point out the practical uses of the computer and to highlight some of its achievements. We should not forget that the computer, which is now an integral part of our everyday lives, has developed in less than a lifetime. Tomorrow? Who knows!

8
Data Processing

Although computers were initially designed to solve scientific problems, the bulk of computing today is concerned with *data processing,* which covers a wide field of applications relating to commercial, governmental and industrial tasks, some of which were outlined in the previous chapter. Data processing "probably accounts for between two-thirds and three-quarters of all computer people".[1] The purpose of discussing data processing is not because so many computer personnel are engaged in this activity, but rather because it brings us back to a major concept, namely that computers *process information.*

So far in this book, the two terms *information* and *data* have been used interchangeably. There is, however, a difference between the two. The digits "070132" constitute data but they convey no information. They could be interpreted as a catalogue number, a date (7th January, '32) or, as is the case, the dialling code from London to Hambledon — 070 132. The objective of data processing is to marshal or organize data into meaningful information. In this chapter we shall investigate what this entails.

DATA PROCESSING

Scientific data processing usually involves a great deal of computation (arithmetical and comparison operations) upon a relatively small amount of input data, resulting in a small volume of output. On the other hand, commercial data processing involves a large volume of input data, relatively few computational operations and a large volume of output. In the early days of computers, the emphasis was upon scientific data processing, but once it was appreciated that the computer was not only a computational tool but also had the ability to store vast amounts of data, then commercial organizations became interested. In the United Kingdom, the J. Lyons Company designed a computer for their own business purposes (LEO) which became operational in 1951. In the United States, also in 1951, the UNIVAC machine, intended for both scientific and commercial applications, was the first machine to be widely used for data processing.

The processing of information existed long before computers. Every organization whether commercial, industrial or governmental, has always had a certain amount of paperwork. Prior to computers, this paperwork would have been processed manually and/or with the help of business machines. Within a computerized data processing system, however, information has to be structured so that, as data, it can be handled by a computer.

We shall now briefly examine the steps by which information (current and past paperwork) is expressed as data, processed, and returned to managers or other individuals, as updated and useful information. There are, basically, five steps:

1) preparation of source documents;
2) input of data;
3) manipulation of data;
4) output of information;
5) storage of data.

Source Documents: The first step is to obtain the relevant facts and figures and to set these out on source documents. For example, in a population survey, the name, address, age, sex, occupation, etc., must be first written down onto a survey sheet or some other document. These documents may be so designed that information is recorded in the same structure as the data required by the computer program.

Data Input: Once the data has been extracted from the source document, it must then be transposed into some form suitable for entry into the computer so that processing can take place. The method will depend upon the input media or device, e.g., punched cards or paper tape, teletypewriters, OCR documents.

Data Manipulation: Information, input as data, for processing, may have to be *classified* or *sorted*. It is this form of operation, or data manipulation, rather than pure computation, with which data processing is mainly concerned. For example, in the population survey, we may want to classify people by occupation or by age. We may wish to sort lists of names or items in alphabetical order; or, in a social service environment, to list people to be visited by street order. We may require employees to be grouped by departments for a payroll program; or, in a job-costing program, to group the costs of all the elements that went into the manufacture of an item. This will involve some form of *calculation,* another example of which is the calculation of a weekly

1. An industrial view as quoted in "Computing Science Review", Science Research Council, June 1972. Page 53, section 9.2.

wage based on the hours worked times the rate of pay. All these forms of data manipulation will produce results, results which can be organized in the form of *summaries,* e.g., the numbers of adults and children in a given district or street, or the numbers of children of school age and of those under school age.

Output of Information: The objective of outputting results or summaries is to provide meaningful information to managers, account-ants, population survey analysts, and so forth. Careful consideration, therefore, should be given to the *presentation* of results so that they can be digested easily and quickly. With the first flush of data processing by computers, everything which could be generated was often printed out, resulting in pages of figures which by their sheer volume became confusing. Even summaries can be hard to read if not clearly laid out. People receiving computer output have been forced to think out more exactly what information they require from the computer and how it can be presented most usefully.

Data Storage: In most cases, the results of processing one set of data are retained for future use or reference. For example, in a payroll program, last week's updated results will be needed by this week's program in order to update the 'gross-pay-to-date' total. In the other examples cited, it may be necessary, after updating, to compare the latest figures with previous figures, perhaps over different periods of time (sales analysis). This means that data processing installations require a great deal of secondary storage space to store all the programs and the different sets of data.

FILES AND RECORDS

Data relating to a specific application, for example, payroll (or inventory

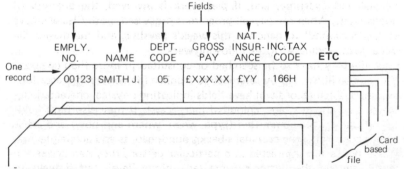

Fig. 8.1 A record, of fixed length and number of fields, may require several cards to contain all the necessary information.

control, sales analysis or invoicing to customers) is organized as a separate *file*. Each file is made up of a number of *records* which, in turn, contain a number of *fields* or *properties*. On a payroll file, comprising the many records of everybody on the staff, each record will have certain fields to represent the individual employee's name and number, department, gross pay, National Insurance contribution, income tax code, etc.

Each record in a given file has the same structure, i.e., the same number of fields, with a given field in each record always containing information about a particular property, e.g., the 4th field always contains "Gross Pay" and the 6th field "Income Tax Code".

There must be some method of being able to select one particular record from all the others. This is possible by choosing one of the fields as a *key*. For example, if the police are interested in the details of a given criminal on their criminal records file, the obvious *key-field* to look under is the criminal-name-field, since this will be unique for each record. Similarly, in a payroll file, the key-field would be the employee-number-field or, in a banking environment, the unique customer's-account-number-field.

Once the initial information (from the source document) has been encoded onto punched cards or paper tape as a file of individual records, this is usually copied onto magnetic tape or disk, so that when the information is required by a program, it can be transferred more speedily into main memory. In the case of direct input via a teletypewriter terminal, the records would go straight onto disk.

It is customary to set up a *master file* of permanent (and, usually, the latest) data, and to use *transaction files* containing data of a temporary nature. For example, the master payroll file will contain not only all the permanent details about each employee, his name and number, income tax code and so forth, but it will also include the current gross-pay-to-date total and the tax paid-to-date total. The transaction payroll file will contain details of hours worked *this* week, normal and overtime, and, if piecework is involved, the quantity of goods made. When the payroll program is processed, both files will have to be 'consulted' to generate this week's payslips, and the master file updated in readiness for the following week.

A file may have to be searched or consulted in more than one way. This can be illustrated by reference to a police file containing records of criminals. Each record will have fields indicating physical characteristics (height, weight, sex, age, colour of hair, scars). It may also have fields to indicate crimes committed (type, when, where and how) and other details concerning the criminal's background, haunts and acquaintances. If the police are interested in a particular person, they can access the master file by the person's name (an unique field), but if they are looking for a type of suspect (e.g., a female, 6ft tall, red hair, over forty), they can access the file by the characteristics of a physical description, using several fields. A search program can scan the records on file and produce a list of all those who fit the required description.

The weakness of some data processing systems is that whilst they work for most of the time and for most situations, the exceptions are overlooked. An effective system should anticipate all likely and foreseeable contingencies. It is necessary to consider in advance very carefully everything that may be required – the amount and type of data and how it may be manipulated – so that the structure of each record will be adequate for *all* circumstances. Files will be updated and amended, but to alter their structure at a later date is usually very troublesome.

The various processes carried out on files may be summarized as follows:

File Creation: This is the method of organizing one's data for use by the computer system into a series of records of a particular length, content and layout.

File Access: When the particular application program is in use, it will have to access the relevant file(s). Since each file may contain a great deal of data, it may not be possible for the entire file to reside in main memory and portions of it will have to be drawn from secondary storage as required. A part of the operating system known as the *file management* system takes care of this activity. It is able to pass a certain number of records into main memory, to know when these have been processed, to transfer them back to the storage device, and to usher in some more.

File Manipulation and Maintenance: Having accessed the file, the individual records will be processed in some way (sorted or classified) but, in addition, other records may have to be added or deleted (a payroll file will need to add and delete employee records as people join or leave the company). In some cases, all the records on file may be printed out; in others, perhaps only selected records would need to be printed.

File Generation: As a result of the manipulation of data in files, new files will be generated. Once an existing file has been altered, it is necessary to create a new file by writing the updated (altered) file on a new tape or another area of disk. The old tape or area of disk can then become available for re-use.

File Organization

The address of a record, that is, its place within the data processing system as a whole, depends upon the type of storage used. In chapter 3 we discussed sequential and direct access. Let us consider these terms again as they relate to file organization.

Sequential: Records on magnetic tape are arranged in a sequential order. The only way to get to a particular record, say the third one, is by passing over the first and second. In other words, the program has to start at the beginning of the file and work through it. This means that the program must "look at", in some sense, each preceding record to see whether it is the one required. This is costly in time when only one, or a few, records need to be accessed and illustrates one disadvantage of magnetic tape. Another is the fact that three or four tapes are required to perform a sorting procedure.

Direct: With the development of magnetic disks and drums, some of the disadvantages of sequential file organization were overcome. Direct file organization enables the program to have immediate access to the record required. The program need only inform the file management system which record is needed and from which file, and the management system then searches through the filing system and produces the record. Because magnetic disks allow direct access, as well as having a faster rate of data transfer, records can be accessed more quickly than is possible for magnetic tape.

Direct file organization is usually the better method when the need is for immediate processing of small quantities of different records at irregular but fairly frequent intervals, i.e., in airline reservations, banking, etc. When entire files, or the majority of records have to be processed (e.g., weekly/monthly payrolls, quarterly stock-takings), it is usually cheaper, and sometimes as fast, to use sequential file organization.

Efficient data processing depends on a clear analysis of what the user requires. How such an analysis is achieved and how the user's objectives can be met is the subject of the next chapter.

9
An Introduction to Systems Analysis

A national newspaper reported "Computer Makes Firm Bankrupt". Such a statement is misleading since it portrays the computer as some malevolent beast wishing harm to its owner. But the fact remains that the company did become bankrupt after installing a computer. We can also quote a computer system in the U.S.A. which recorded details about every suspect (innocent or guilty) picked up by the police. If a person was 'booked' again, at a later date, details of any previous criminal record would be readily available. This system, however, failed to delete information when a suspect was *not* convicted. Thus any policeman checking through the file could be given useless, and possibly prejudicial, information about innocent people. Why do these situations arise and how can they be avoided? We cannot blame the computer, nor can we always blame the programmer.

There is one large area within the computing process which has not yet been discussed. People tend to think of there being a problem (payroll, control of traffic) which is tossed to a programmer with a curt "Now go away and make the computer do it." The procedure is not as simple as this. Just as we saw that the computer is surrounded by an intricate web of software, so the procedure for computerizing a problem is made more complex by a large area which we shall call 'para-computing' (see Fig. 9.1), and of which *systems analysis* forms the major part. One of its main functions is to convert an existing manual system into a computerized system. The systems analyst does so by defining in broad outline how the problem in the outside world is to be related to a computer system. It is from this framework that the programmer works. If the outline has been poorly designed, the type of situations described above can easily occur.

THE DEVELOPMENT OF SYSTEMS ANALYSIS

Systems analysis is a recent discipline whose development goes back to the late 1950's, at which time commercial organizations began to make use of computers with especial success in one area, namely, company payrolls. We know that a computer requires accurate and detailed

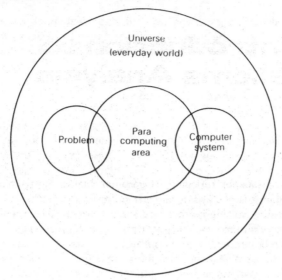

Fig. 9.1 In addition to Systems Analysis, para-computing also includes Data
      Collection and Data Preparation.

information before it can carry out a task successfully. Since the
payroll procedure, as a manual system, was so clearly defined, it was a
relatively simple matter for a programmer to convert the payroll
procedure into a program. However, difficulties emerged when the same
programmers were asked to computerize other parts of a business
system which were less clearly defined, for example, stock control, sales
forecasting. They could perform the programming, but not the process
of converting a manual system into a form in which it could be
programmed.

The main difficulty in any routine business application is not so
much what to do in normal circumstances, but how to tackle all the
exceptions to the rule. If a computerized system only takes into
account customers' orders sent through the post and ignores the
possibility of orders placed over the telephone, then these latter 'input'
orders will never be processed. Most business systems are not
documented fully enough for computerization. All the exceptions are
known by the office staff involved, and they know what to do when
these arise. The precise investigation and formulation of *all* aspects of a
business system to the level needed for computerization has become a
separate speciality performed by a *systems analyst*. A successful analyst
is one who can study the manual system, looking for not only the
normal procedures but also the abnormal situations, and can then build
these into an overall computer system. He has evolved as the interface
between the company and the computer system.

There are two stages in the work of an analyst. First, he performs a detailed analysis of the existing system and then he designs a computerized system based upon the analysis. We shall now discuss the work of the analyst in more detail.

The Analyst's Relationship to the Company

One of the primary activities of the analyst within the company is to communicate with top management. The decisions about what will be computerized, and to what extent, will have to be taken by management in the light of the report, or *feasibility study,* presented to them by the systems analyst. At this stage, the analyst is only concerned with helping management to make the correct decisions.

The analyst will have to work with every department in the company which might be affected by computerization. No new system can hope to be successful until its effect on other departments has been carefully measured. To do this, the analyst has to *gather information* from the company's personnel and here, of course, the problem of human relations is raised. Some workers may think that the systems analyst is trying to replace them with a computer! It is not unknown for false information to be deliberately given because of this fear. At the very least, the work done by the analyst results in changes of working practices and conditions which could lead to problems with individuals, trade unions and so on. Tact, a maturity of understanding, and an ability to *communicate* with people are essential to the analyst.

He has to meet both management and company personnel to present a clear explanation of their new role arising out of computerization. This includes educating or retraining people in their 'new' practices, even down to the level of explaining why some documents carry the legend "do not fold, staple or bend" (the machine will not accept them, or they damage the machine).

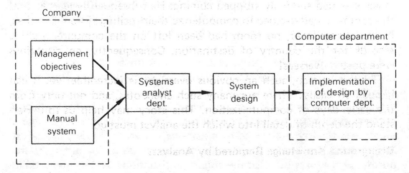

Fig. 9.2 Inter-relationship of the Analyst's Work between the Company and the Computer Department.

The Analyst's Relationship to the Computer Department

Although the systems analyst is often found working within the computer department, conceptually his duties place him in a position midway between the company and the data processing department. He has to rely on the computer manager, the programmers and other DP (data processing) staff to carry out his systems design. Good relations with the department are therefore important, and friction could occur if it is not clear who is responsible for the following issues:

— the choice of programming language;
— keeping within the schedule and budget;
— who may contact client departments directly about details in records.

Communication between the analysts and the rest of the company, particularly the programmers, requires *formal documentation*. This simply means a highly detailed record of what the systems design must achieve and how this is to be carried out. The precision of detail required is something only fully appreciated by the people actually involved. For example, if columns 30—35 of a certain record are used as a field to enter a worker's gross weekly wage, then the program will interpret what is found in these columns as the gross wage, even if the man's date of birth has been placed there in error. Formal documentation serves not only to show the programmer for what purpose certain columns are to be used, but also the other departments who have to fill them in, and it also indicates how they are to do so. Any flaw in this documentation can have disastrous results. One small example may illustrate this point.

An American mail order firm sent magazines not only to their home market but also abroad. One English recipient was surprised to find his magazines had suddenly stopped coming. He subsequently learned that the company had decided to computerize their mailing system and that, in the change over, no room had been left on the computer address records for the country of destination. Consequently, no magazines were posted overseas!

To the layman, such an obvious oversight is incredible: yet it can happen so easily. There are many such anecdotes, and not only from the early days of computerization. This story may help us to understand the depth of detail into which the analyst must go.

Background Knowledge Required by Analysts

A wide background knowledge of both business methods and computing is essential to the systems analyst. No one person can be expected to be skilled in all fields and there is a tendency today, in large companies, to re-define systems analysis into two roles. The *business* analyst who specifies the system design (in non-technical terms) and the *technical* analyst who takes the specification and assumes responsibility for the design problems associated with the computer system.

The business analyst would have to be familiar with some of the following subjects: business structure, organization, management and administration; production planning and control; stores and stock control; accounting; operational (operations) research; conducting and analyzing surveys; simulation and model building. Whereas the technical analyst should possess a knowledge of the techniques of data processing, programming, computer operations, computer systems (including the current cost and performance of both hardware and software); and he should be able to advise on the relative merits of I/O and secondary storage most appropriate to the company's needs.

INITIATING A SYSTEM

Suppose you are in a non-computerized organization, or that you have a problem which could benefit from the use of a computer. Where do you begin to find out whether you really need a computer, which system, or what hardware and software to use? You would approach a systems analyst, either through your own DP department or through one of the consultancy agencies.

Let us now draw up a possible, and admittedly ideal, framework showing the sequence of events which takes place when a computer system is proposed. The steps involved are:

1) assignment brief;
2) steering committee;
3) feasibility study;
4) full system investigation;
5) design, implementation and testing.

Assignment Brief

Top management briefs the systems analyst as to the objectives of the proposed system. It provides the necessary authorization for him to investigate files, to enter other departments and question personnel, and assigns company staff to help the analyst in his investigation.

Steering Committee

The analyst must meet and discuss the overall objectives given by top management with other members of staff. This is done in committee with the managers of all the departments involved, the analyst and, if one has been appointed, the DP manager.

Feasibility Study

As the name implies, it is a survey of the possibility of computerization based on management's objectives related to an analysis of the existing facilities within the company. The resultant analyst's proposal may be to go ahead with computerization; *not* to go ahead (i.e., the existing system would not benefit by computerization — honesty is required here by analysts, especially if brought in from an outside organization); or, to defer the matter because it is impractical at the present time. Feasibility studies tie down company personnel so they are concluded as speedily as possible and, whatever the decision, the analysts have to be paid. If the survey concludes that a computerized system is not necessary, or that the original objectives are not attainable, the reasons are clearly stated, but if it appears that a computer system is feasible, the study will bring out the following points:

a) What are the likely problem areas which will need special attention?
b) What are the likely computer configurations which would be suitable?
c) What are these configurations likely to cost in terms of money, staff and time — to design, to install, to test, and to run?

Full System Investigation

If management concludes that it should go ahead with a particular system, or further explore several alternatives, the systems analyst will then prepare a detailed design, or several proposals, which must be complete in every probable and possible detail. Failure to do so will court disaster. It should be emphasized that once a particular system has been selected, one tends to become tied to it. It is often impractical to change a system drastically at a later stage. The analyst should insure that what appears to be practical now will be capable of providing, or incorporating, the possible modifications that subsequently may be required.

Design, Implementation and Testing

Most computer systems are implemented on a modular basis, i.e., the overall design system will be broken down into a series of sub-units (modules), each one being thoroughly tested before becoming operational. As each module proves to be satisfactory it will be integrated into the developing overall system. Ideally, both the manual and the computerized systems should run together side by side until everyone concerned is satisfied that "all the bugs have been ironed out." This is expensive and does not always happen. When it does, the kind of nightmares described earlier are invariably avoided.

* * *

The most important point to be appreciated from this chapter is that for successful computerization, the process cannot be left entirely to the computing professionals. A dialogue must exist between the computer specialists and those directly involved. With the right kind of dialogue, computerization cannot but help all concerned. A respected doctor/lawyer is one who, amongst other things, takes the trouble to *explain* an illness/problem to his patient/client. Strikes are better resolved when both sides really understand each other's problems (and fears). When it is a question of computerizing some system which affects the whole of society (e.g., the collation of all known facts about an individual in one central file — the privacy issue, and see chapter 11), then it is essential for everybody concerned to be involved in the discussion.

10

The Organization of a Data Processing Department

If it is decided that your organization is to become computerized, you will require the services of a data processing (DP) department. The personnel involved may be as many as a thousand or as few as half-a-dozen. The number obviously affects the structure of the department. Many a small business has insufficient work to justify the expense of installing its own system but still requires access to a computer. Computer bureaux, which hire out time on a contract basis, have grown up to meet this situation. Whether the data processing is handled internally (within the company) or externally (by a bureau) there are three major areas in which personnel are involved; design, development and operation.

DESIGN (Systems Analysis)

In the previous chapter we discussed the role of the systems analyst. In a large organization there may be a group of such analysts, headed by a *senior systems analyst* who would be primarily concerned with establishing the need for a computer based system and, subsequently, for directing its design. The analyst and/or his team (who may function outside the DP department), would prepare detailed specifications of the problem in a form suitable for the programming staff to interpret. The senior analyst would draw up plans, maybe in block diagram form, outlining the main sections of the computer solution. His colleagues in the group would then expand these in much more detail.

Before a system can become operational, the systems analyst arranges trial runs with suitable test data. It may be necessary to organize courses and to prepare instruction manuals to explain to personnel the procedures for the collection and preparation of data. Once a project is implemented, continual assessment is necessary to insure that the system continues to meet the original specifications.

DEVELOPMENT (Programming)

Most organizations who require computer services will need a *suite* or range of several programs, e.g., covering payroll, stock control, production control, customer accounts, and other operations. These may be provided as packages by the manufacturer, but if they have to be developed in-house, the production of such a suite of programs must be completed within an acceptable period of time by a group of programmers working together as a team, with each member being responsible for one part or sub-section of the entire project. For this to work efficiently, certain overall standards have to be agreed and conscientiously followed by all members of the programming group.

A large team would be led by a *programming manager* who would specify individual responsibilities as well as the time-scale for each stage of development. In addition, the programming manager would be responsible for the efficiency of the operating system software.

There are two levels of programmers; production or applications programmers, and systems programmers.

The *applications programmer* works from the outline design provided by the analyst and follows the plan of operation laid down by the programming manager. He is concerned with the construction of a step-by-step solution, the subsequent coding and program testing. He is likely to work in a high-level language, e.g. COBOL for a commercial program.

The *systems programmer* is concerned with the maintenance and development of the operating system software. It may be that an installation can rely almost entirely on the system software supplied by the manufacturer but, in all probability, it will be necessary to modify this software to suit the special requirements of the environment in which it is being used. In contrast to the applications programmer, the systems programmer must have a knowledge of the language of the machine which will be used.

OPERATIONS

The day-to-day running of a computer system will entail the operation of the equipment, the preparation of data and the distribution of computer output, and the manual control of files.

Computer operators are responsible for controlling and monitoring the progress of programs through the computer system. This may involve setting up magnetic tapes on the tape drives, changing disk packs, loading card decks, supplying the printer and terminals with paper, cleaning tape drives and disks, and other such routine maintenance. They must be able to recognize unusual behaviour or technical problems within the system and decide on appropriate action, and they will usually keep log-books recording machine use and behaviour. The operating system is able to provide information about the computer's performance and this may be displayed on a VDU device generally sited at a central point in the computer room and known as an operator's console.

Data has to be input to the system, e.g. keying-to-tape or disk, or via a teletypewriter terminal, or data has to be prepared for input to the system, e.g. cards and paper tape will be punched and verified. In some installations, usually those which have many external users, additional staff will be concerned with the control of data. For example, they may be needed to collect data from several branches or departments, or to collect data over variable periods of time (e.g., daily input for weekly/ monthly reports), and then to assemble it for processing. This section would also be concerned with the distribution of output to the different departments within an organization, or even to external customers (e.g. computer generated bills and statements). Responsibility may extend to checking the validity of data and also the accuracy of output.

In installations where large quantities of data need to be retained, there may be a *file librarian* who is concerned with classifying and cataloguing the various files according to their contents and use, and also with the physical storage of the many reels of magnetic tape (or removable disk packs) which would be required in such an installation.

The operating group of a computer installation usually operates at least two shifts per day together with partial weekend work. An installation may even work twenty-four hours a day, seven days a week in order to provide the services that are required. The expense of a large computer system may be such that the system is only viable if it operates as near to capacity as possible.

The *operations manager* will need to organize the necessary staff and to schedule the workload. He will need to consider job priority and special computing requirements. For example, the payroll program must never be allowed to run late, and a program which requires the line printer for a lengthy period of time (very heavy output) may have to be run at off-peak hours, during the night. However tight the work schedule may be, time must also be set aside for the regular maintenance of equipment, particularly the major maintenance which will normally be handled by engineers from the computer manufacturer.

The organization and deployment of personnel within a DP department will be determined by the amount and type of work that it handles or plans to handle, by the variation of computing equipment in use and proposed, and by the range of computing power that may be available now and in the future. The overall responsibility for the department will rest in the hands of the *data processing manager.*

The DP manager will be involved in the planning and implementation of new projects as well as in controlling existing systems. He will need to work closely with other departments which will be affected. He will draw up procedural methods and standards for the guidance of his staff, and he will oversee their recruitment, training and welfare. He will also be concerned with security, not only of the installation itself, but also the security and control of the libraries of data and program files of all users.

A data processing department may be small or large. In a small department, personnel may have several duties, even to the extent of the manager being involved in systems analysis, writing programs and operating the computer. Irrespective of a department's size, the data processing manager will need to be a businessman as well as a computer expert. He will be concerned with budgets, personnel and equipment. He must be alert to the current needs of the department's users, his clients, and keep himself up-to-date on developments in software and hardware so that he can maintain, and hopefully improve, the high level of efficiency which is required of a DP department.

The use of computers involves a heavy and continuing investment in money, time and skills. A computer system, therefore, should be both efficient and *reliable*. A breakdown could entail not merely widespread inconvenience and discomfort, but in some cases it could be a matter affecting life and death, e.g., in air traffic control and in certain medical applications. As we have seen in Chapter 6, such systems would have back-up facilities to insure continuity of service. However, it is important in *all* systems that emergency prodecures be set up, understood and strictly followed by everyone concerned. System faults need to be corrected promptly and, where possible, a system should be designed so that a fault in one piece of equipment does not necessarily mean the stoppage of the entire installation.

Computing will usually be a corporate undertaking requiring a disciplined and well-ordered approach from the design stage through to successful completion of a project.

Computer management must harness and combine the many specialized talents which are essential for efficient data processing. In a large installation it will be necessary to organize the various processes into formal departments and sub-departments, the structure of which might look as follows:

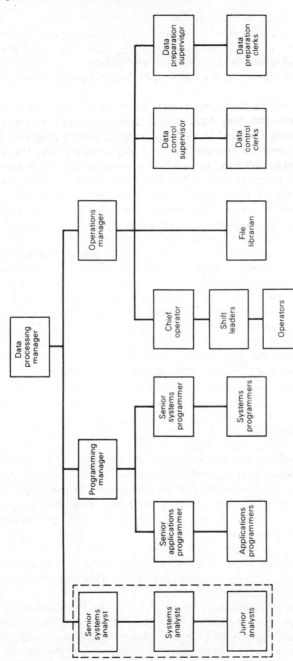

Fig. 10.1 Organization of a Data Processing Department. Note that the analyst group may function outside the DP department.

11
The Social Issues

We have seen that computers can be used to store, up-date and analyze information, to direct and control industrial processes, and to aid and encourage scientific research. These, and many other applications, have brought about many changes in the organization and quality of life which affect us directly as individuals or indirectly as members of society. There has been little time in which to adjust to these changes and much more time will need to pass before we can fully appreciate the potential benefits and dangers of computerization.

Whatever the use to which computers are applied, there is always a social implication. Whether the computer is used as a clerk to prepare bills, as an information system to provide medical records or credit-worthiness, in the control of traffic or industrial processes, in management, education or design, or in scientific research and analysis, there are issues involving *people* and such emotive words as automation, redundancy, privacy, security, impersonalization and individuality come to the fore.

Information Processing

Speedy and efficient information processing is crucial to our socially conscious and highly developed technological society. Computers have helped to reduce the intolerable burden of handling the ever increasing amount of information with which government departments, public services and business concerns are expected to contend. Having eased the problem, computers, because of their ability to analyze information as well as to retain, up-date and reproduce it, and, because of their versatility to present it in a variety of forms, have exacerbated the information explosion and we could not cope with today's volume of information without computers.

The availability of information on the scale that computers have made possible has brought many positive benefits. In law or in medicine, for example, access to a mass of information, which it is only possible to search through or analyze quickly enough with the aid of a computer, may benefit clients and patients. In addition, information from the past relating to many other subjects can now be gathered together and used for predicting future patterns so that more reliable decisions of future behaviour can be made in many areas, whether scientific or sociological, private or public.

Efficiency/Productivity

If we equate the efficiency of a process in terms of its cost, speed and accuracy of output, there is ample evidence in industrial applications that the introduction of the computer has brought positive results. In process control the use of the computer frequently leads to increased efficiency in terms of minimizing wastage and/or raising the quality of output (paper mills, steel) which more than compensates for what may indeed be very high computing costs. It may also raise the safety level of a process (chemical plants), a benefit which is beyond measure in terms of money.

There are applications in which time is critical, apart from considerations of cost and safety. In the design of a large engineering project, such as a power station or dam, many inter-related factors have to be taken into account, the assessment of which involves very many lengthy calculations. This would require many people working over many months and, because of the wide possibilities for human error, experimental models would have to be built, tested, and modified — a costly, slow process. By the time the right answer had been found, the project may be too late or out-of-date. It may have become uneconomic because of rising costs during the lengthy design period. With computers it is possible to create mathematical models which can simulate the actual and likely conditions so that the problems can be solved quickly and economically enough so that implementation of a project is practicable.

In business and commerce the efficiency claim is well founded. A large part of business operations involves non-creative, routine clerical tasks and the computer can handle a great volume of such tasks more quickly, more accurately and more reliably than is possible manually.

Organizations, large or small, do not thrive or fail because of the presence or absence of a computer, but because of the quality of the people who run them. The larger an organization, the more likely it is to be a candidate for computerization. Computer links between head office, local branches and allied companies have several effects. The local branch or allied company gains access to a wider range of opportunities, it can buy and sell more economically, offer additional services or better terms and, generally, become more efficient and competitive. Customers appreciate this, but the competing small shop on the corner or local family business will feel itself jeopardized by a remote giant. At head office the computer makes it easier to centralize control and to explore even larger, new horizons. This can lead to streamlining and greater efficiency on the one hand but, on the other, it can lead to a loss of consideration for the individual and for local needs.

The computer can provide many advantages but we must insure that those advantages are not abused. Any computer system must be so conceived and operated that it is man who runs the machine and can adapt it to his changing needs. The machine cannot be allowed to determine the patterns of our lives, and those of us who enjoy its benefits automatically acquire the responsibility for insuring that it is used as wisely and as humanely as possible.

Automation

The object of bringing in a computer, or of extending existing computer facilities, may be to increase productivity, to attain a consistently high quality of product, to improve a service and/or to gain knowledge. It may be to extend an existing manual system, perhaps to increase the speed and efficiency of operation, or to handle more work without increasing staff or accommodation, or to provide management with information more quickly.

In most cases it will also be hoped to keep current and future costs down. Computers and computing, very expensive though they often are, can, in many cases, achieve these goals. In the process they can eliminate a lot of drudgery — and jobs, boring though they may be. But in the majority of applications computers rarely eliminate, and can never *economically* replace, human judgement. By eliminating drudgery they should free us for more creative endeavours and the exercise of values that are peculiarly human. However, those who fear, rightly or wrongly, that they are likely to lose their jobs because of computers are naturally sceptical of the advantages of computerization.

In business and commerce the computer has complemented rather than replaced the work force. Jobs may have been lost in one area but, because of the many tasks involved in the collection and handling of information, they have been re-created in another. In industrial situations the computer has taken over many routine, semi-skilled jobs, some of which were also hazardous, and it has offered in their place more rewarding jobs. But, in whatever environment, the new jobs are likely to be of a more technical nature than those which have been replaced. The use of computer technology has also helped to create new products and services, and hence new jobs. The re-training of personnel for the new, more highly skilled jobs, or for jobs in another industry, is a very important issue.

Privacy/Individuality

Data processing has expanded the amount of information (present and past) which is available. We can make use of this in more efficient, productive and automated ways, but what is the implication for the person who is providing the basic information on which these processes are taking place?

Whilst there may be administrative, and even social, advantages in compiling and retaining computer files relating to such things as employment details, tax payments, education, health records, bank accounts and credit-worthiness, such files may contain facts which, as individuals, we consider very sensitive. It is important that this personal information is handled with care and is not available to those who do not require it. If computer systems are correctly designed, unsolicited access to information is prevented. In fact, the information may well be a good deal safer on a computer file than in the traditional filing cabinet.

As long as the files remain available only to those immediately concerned, all seems fairly reasonable. What is unpalatable is the thought of centralized files in large data banks being cross-referenced to create detailed, individual dossiers. It is the idea of the drawing together of information from different sources which is the crux of the privacy problem. It gives rise to the fear of the machine being used, or abused, for purposes of surveillance.

Whilst it can be argued that for reasons of efficiency, convenience and economy, information systems *should* be combined and shared, equal consideration should be given to insure that such action does not lead to an infringement of individual privacy.

Security

Computer users themselves have a similar concern that their data banks are not made available to, or can be damaged by, unauthorized persons. Trade and defence secrets must be protected (like individual medical and pay records) against unwarranted exposure and, indeed, sabotage by actual or potential rivals or mischief makers. The threat to security of information, and the threat to individual privacy, are counter arguments for making information systems too widely interchangeable. But if security and privacy are valuable, they are, in computing as elsewhere, qualities which are expensive to achieve and they require continuous maintenance.

Laws for the protection of information and of privacy have been in existence since before the days of computers. The recent and growing information explosion requires government, and the public at large, to extend its vigilance so that laws, checks and controls are established as necessary for the continued protection of all.

Although we have become very dependent on computers, they, like ourselves, are very vulnerable. We have to make sure that the computers themselves are protected so that they can provide the benefits, the power and the knowledge which they offer us. Their security is our security.

CONCLUSIONS/FUTURE

Society is already more computerized than many people may imagine and because of the implications of this, some of which we have examined, it is clearly important that people become aware of the potentialities so that they can seek to influence future use. Awareness hinges on education and this is growing and must continue to expand — hopefully, at the same fast pace at which the youthful, vigorous computer industry is itself expanding.

In the final analysis, man is shaped by his own tools. What of the motor car? Many benefits have undoubtedly been derived from this invention, but the consequences wrought on society have been far reaching, and they were unforeseeable in the first instance. The increased mobility provided by the automobile has helped to alter the very structure of family life. Roads and motorways have scarred the face of the land, and increasing traffic accidents and pollution have brought suffering to motorists and non-motorists alike.

Inevitably, the computer seems destined to bring radical changes and some of these we may not yet have appreciated as potential problems. The goal, surely, is not to create a better world of computers, but to create a better world for man to live in. There may be conflict in balancing 'progress' with 'civilization' and, in the long run, society can only blame itself if computers are allowed to create more problems than they solve. What is happening to the under-developed countries? Are computers helping to close, or to widen, the gap between those who have and those who have not? In China, for example, it is expected that computers and semiconductor technology [1] will play a leading role in helping to transform the country into a modern advanced technological society.

The Industrial Revolution saw many technological developments, the social effects of which have changed over several generations before becoming absorbed into our way of life. Significant changes have taken place in the twenty-five years since the computer industry came into being, but several lifetimes may have to pass before the social and cultural effects of the computer are fully realized.

What of tomorrow's world? The advance of the micro-electronics industry has provided a new impetus to an already rapidly moving computer industry. Computers will become cheaper, easier to handle and more widely available to the general public. This will affect our lives as individuals and the societies in which we live. We may well be on our way to becoming an automated society. It is even suggested that the office girl will have to make way for the automatic word processor.

Probably the greatest impact the computer can have on the availability and usefulness of information is still to be felt. Access to computer stored information from within the home is already a reality and once commercial quantities of the television attachments needed are available to the general public at a cost they can readily afford, the effect on life is likely to be quite profound.

A teletext compatible TV set, besides providing all normal programs, can transmit pages of up to the minute news and other specialized information at the touch of a button, e.g. general news items, weather reports, entertainments lists, summaries of fresh food prices in the shops, state of the pound and trade figures. The number of pages available at present is limited, but the British Post Office development, a viewdata type service, is on a potentially much larger scale, enabling the provision of more comprehensive details and on a wider range of specialized subjects. It will not only make it possible to summon any of thousands of pages of text through a "phone-TV set" link but will also provide the means of talking back to the computer and sending information, e.g. perhaps even ordering and arranging for the payment of goods. It is expected that the service will also be of considerable benefit to business organizations as a means of providing up-to-date information and improving internal communications.

The true significance of a universally available information service which can be used without any prior knowledge of computers and without any training is difficult to assess. It has the potential to be the most powerful and useful information retrieval system so far invented.

What will result from research into *machine intelligence*[2]? The development of robots to work in certain hostile situations, such as fire-fighting, mines, security of sensitive establishments, and space exploration, could bring considerable benefits. The industrial robot, with the potential to lead to automation on a scale not yet envisaged or understood, may not be so socially acceptable.

1. See appendix 1.
2. The aim is to create machines that can think and act in much the same way as human beings. The extent to which development can take place depends on solving many problem areas such as getting machines to 'see' objects, to distinguish objects by touch, to recognize spoken words in the many different ways they can be pronounced, to learn to imitate intelligent behaviour, and ultimately to combine these achievements into an integrated system as with human beings. *Artificial intelligence* and *robotics* are names given to the same branch of computing. As an example of 'intelligence', programs have been written to enable the computer to play chess.

What seems certain is that many fields of human endeavour will become more dependent on computers and this will inevitably lead to a widening of horizons which were previously unimaginable. Satellites have made the world smaller. A space shot recorded snow patterns of the Himalayas and it is said that this could lead to the development of large-scale irrigation schemes of incalculable benefit to the arid regions of the sub-continent of India. The real significance is that we are on the threshold of new discoveries and new worlds previously beyond man's comprehension.

APPENDICES

1
The Development of Computers

The computer evolved as a result of man's search for fast, accurate calculating devices. However, the birth of computers depended upon many other factors, such as the acceleration of certain technological improvements from the early 1900's, the availability of vast sums of money for computer development as a result of World War II, changes in government attitudes, and the evolution of basic computing theories as developed by von Neumann,[1] Shannon[2] and Turing.[3] It is hoped that this appendix will be of interest for its own sake as well as affording a background knowledge of the development of computers. Essentially, there are three kinds of calculating devices; manual, mechanical and automatic.

Manual devices include the abacus, in evidence in the Tigris-Euphrates Valley c. 3500 BC, and, John Napier's bone or cardboard multiplication calculator designed in the early 17th century. It is interesting to note that adapted versions of Napier's invention were still being manufactured in 1888 and in the Far East today the abacus is still in use.

Mechanical devices include Blaise Pascal's adding machine (1642) and Gottfried Wilhelm von Leibnitz's stepped calculator (1694). It was not until the early 19th century that the principles of these machines were used with any commercial success. They have changed little since that period. It was left to the genius of Charles Babbage, born in Totnes, Devonshire in 1791, to design a machine which was to be the forerunner of the electronic computer as we know it today. The Analytical Engine has already been discussed in detail in chapter 1 where it was remarked that precision engineering required to manufacture the machine was not available in Babbage's day.

Many years were to pass before Babbage's dream was realized. During the late nineteenth and early twentieth centuries, a great deal of activity took place in the field of punched-card tabulating systems. We shall investigate this briefly since it has a direct bearing upon the development of the computer industry.

TABULATING MACHINES

Following the 1880 population census, the United States Census Bureau realized that, with the growth in population, its existing methods of tabulating and analyzing the ten-yearly U.S. National Census had become totally inadequate. Hermann Hollerith, born in 1860, devised a system based on the principle of punching holes onto cards, similar to Jacquard's idea. As a result of a competition held between Hollerith's system and two rival (non-mechanized) systems, he gained a contract to supply his equipment for the 1890 census. It involved the punching of 56 million cards, and his system proved to be a great success. International interest was quickly aroused and the punched card system emerged.

Austria used the system for its December 1890 Census. The New York Central Railroad were the first to attempt a commercial application by using the system for office accounting as early as 1895. For this particular application, Hollerith had to provide a tabulator with the ability to add rather than merely count, and he based its design on an electromagnetic version of the Leibnitz stepped wheel.

In 1896, Hollerith formed his own company, the Tabulating Machine Company, which he sold in 1911. It merged with two other companies to form the Computing-Tabulating-Recording Company. By 1924, this company became the International Business Machines Corporation, the largest manufacturer, even today, of punched card equipment.

During the years between 1920 and 1930, the punched card system developed steadily, not only in the States but also in Britain and Europe. One of the earliest applications in the U.K. was in the field of astronomy. It concerned the work of Dr. L.J. Comrie of the British Nautical Almanac Office, who in 1926 computed the future positions of the moon at twelve hourly intervals for the period 1935-2000. This he did using a Burroughs Accounting Machine in conjunction with Hollerith punched cards. An estimated half a million cards were used in this mammoth calculation.

THE ADVENT OF DIGITAL COMPUTERS

Harvard Mark 1

In 1937, Howard A. Aiken of Harvard University, using the

1. John von Neumann's contribution is discussed later in this appendix.
2. In 1938, Claude Shannon noticed that Boole's algebra (developed in 1845) could be used for describing relay and switching circuits.
3. Alan Turing developed the theory of a machine for solving almost any arithmetical problem. If Turing's theoretical machine could not solve a problem, then no computer, however sophisticated, could solve it.

techniques already developed for punched card machinery, began work on the design of a fully automatic calculating machine in collaboration with the International Business Machines Corporation. His aim was to develop a machine which would help him in the solution of complex differential equations, the vast calculations of which would have been impractical manually.

Seven years later, in May 1944, the designs became a reality. In August of the same year, the now historically famous HARVARD MARK I was donated to Harvard University in Cambridge, Massachusetts where it was initially used for classified work for the U.S. Navy.

It had taken technology over a century to catch up with the ideas first mooted by Charles Babbage in Cambridge, England in 1833, but once having achieved this, a phenomenal rate of development followed. Much of value was gained from the research surrounding a project mounted on such a lavish scale as the MARK I. Significantly, the machine proved to be extremely reliable and it remained in active use at Harvard for fifteen years.

The MARK I, or Automatic Sequence Controlled Calculator as it was sometimes called, was complex in design and huge in size. Physically, the machine measured fifty-one feet in length and eight feet in height. It is said to have contained three-quarters of a million parts and in construction to have used more than five hundred miles of wire. It was capable of performing five basic operations; addition, subtraction, multiplication, division and table reference. It was extremely slow by present-day standards but, nevertheless, its realization represented a remarkable achievement. The addition of two numbers took 0.3 of a second and multiplication 4.5 seconds. The magnitude of a number was restricted to twenty-three decimal digits.

The store of the machine consisted of a number of registers each of which was made up of a number of counter wheels. Operating instructions were fed to the computer, not via punched cards, but on punched tape. Each instruction was divisible into two parts; that which specified the type of operation, and that which indicated the storage location where the number to be operated upon was to be found and re-stored in its new form. Information for processing (data) was fed to the machine chiefly by way of punched cards, though values could also be entered by depressing switches manually. Results from processing appeared in punched card form or were typed by an electric typewriter. The MARK I was really an electro-mechanical machine in that its CPU depended on both mechanical and electronic devices for its operation.

ENIAC

The innovation of very high speed vacuum tube switching devices led to the first all-electronic computer, the Electronic Numerical Integrator and Calculator, formally dedicated on 15th February, 1946, only two years after the MARK I. ENIAC was constructed at the Moore School of Engineering of the University of Pennsylvania by a design team led by Professors Eckert and Mauchly.

Achievements were most impressive. In a single hour ENIAC could accomplish calculations which would have taken MARK I one week to perform. The addition of two numbers was achieved in 200 micro-seconds, and multiplication in 2,800 microseconds.

The machine was small in terms of storage capacity and, as it was designed for a specific purpose (ballistics), its use was limited. However, whatever the shortcomings of ENIAC, it represented an impressive feat of electronic engineering.

Von Neumann

Before the completion of ENIAC, a significant event occurred. This was the publication of a paper — "Theory and Techniques of Electronic Digital Computers" by Dr John von Neumann,[4] a consultant to the ENIAC project. The paper represented the first attempt to analyze the problem of computer design in logical terms and it undoubtedly had an enormous impact, for it has since influenced considerably the development of the modern digital computer. Von Neumann's most significant concept was that of the *stored program.* This embodied the idea that a sequence of instructions might be held in the *store* of the computer for the purpose of directing the flow of operations, and that these instructions themselves might then be altered and manipulated in much the same way as data. EDVAC, the Electronic Discrete Variable Automatic Computer, was to be such a machine.

EDVAC

EDVAC made use of acoustic delay lines consisting of tanks of mercury in which the trains of pulses representing data circulated and re-circulated until required to be operated upon by the arithmetic unit. Both the instructions and the numbers to be used for calculation were stored in the memory unit.

There were engineering difficulties during the development stage some, no doubt, attributable to the departure of Eckert and Mauchly who left to form their own computer manufacturing company.[5] In the end, EDVAC was not the first practical computer to operate with an internally stored program. This distinction fell to the British development, EDSAC.

4. In some sources, the credit for the paper is attributed solely to von Neumann, but it seems likely that Eckert and Mauchly were also deeply involved.
5. See page 135.

Manchester Mark I

The earliest stored program computer to operate was probably the small experimental machine built at Manchester University and is generally claimed to have run its first program in June 1948. Its storage capacity, only 32 words, each of 31 binary digits to store data, instructions and working, was too limited to be of any practical use.

The Manchester project was set up by Professor M.H.A. Newman, aided by I.J. Good, F.C. Williams and T. Kilburn. As the latter two claim in a paper, the machine "was built primarily to test the soundness of the storage principle employed (i.e. the Williams-tube type of electrostatic store) and to permit experience to be gained with this type of machine before embarking on the design of a full-size machine". Brian Randell points out[6] part of the interest in the Manchester project is that it does not apparently descend solely from the work at the Moore School.

EDSAC

Work on EDSAC, the Electronic Delay Storage Automatic Calculator, was started early in 1947, in the Cambridge University Mathematical Laboratory by a team under the leadership of Professor Maurice Wilkes who had previously spent some time in the States with the EDVAC team. The machine executed its first program in May 1949. It employed a mercury delay line storage system with an access time of one millisecond. Addition was accomplished in 1,500 microseconds, and multiplication in 4,000 microseconds. The electronic, stored-program, digital computer, as we know it today, had arrived!

COMPUTER 'GENERATIONS'

There is no clear cut pattern of development after EDSAC emerged. The history is tied up in a tangle of technological advances, university research and company amalgamations. What is evident is that the computer industry, as such, did not establish itself until a good deal of the problems had been ironed out on the early prototype projects, and until improvements in components made it cost-effective to produce machines for general use and, also, until industry, commerce and government departments recognized the value of using computers.

In order to simplify matters and at the same time provide a framework for the growth of the computer industry, we shall look at the so-called 'generations' of computers. The custom of referring to the computer era in terms of generations came into wide use after 1964. Although there is a certain amount of overlapping between the generations, the following approximate dates are generally accepted:

| GEN-ERA-TION | COMPONENTS | | SECONDARY STORAGE | SOFTWARE |
	electronic time/operation	central memory time/access		
1st	vacuum tubes. 0.1-1.0 milli-sec.	electrostatic tubes, delay lines. 1 milli-sec.	paper tape, punched cards, delay lines.	none.
2nd	transistors. 1-10 micro-sec.	magnetic drum, magnetic core. 1-10 micro-sec.	magnetic tapes, disks, drums and cards.	subroutine libraries, batch monitors, special I/O hardware
3rd	integrated circuits. 0.1-1.0 micro-sec.	magnetic core and other magnetic media: 0.1-10 micro-sec.	as for 2nd gen. + extended core storage, mass core storage.	same as 2nd gen. + multi-access time-sharing, multi-programming,
late 3rd	as for 3rd gen.	semiconductor registers. 0.1 micro-sec.	as for 3rd gen.	central file systems, relocation, linking, virtual storage, text editors.

Fig. A1.1 Computer 'generations'

1st generation	— 1940-1952
2nd generation	— 1952-1964
3rd generation	— 1964-present
late 3rd generation	— 1968-present

Originally, the term 'generation' was used to distinguish between varying hardware technologies. Since 1968, it has been extended to include both the hardware and the software, which together make up an entire system.

The *first generation* of computers was marked by the use of vacuum tubes for the electronic components and by the use of either electro-static tubes (CRT) or mercury delay lines for storage. Examples of such first generation machines are EDSAC (operational in 1949), SEAC (1950, the first stored program computer operational in the U.S.), EDVAC (1951) and IAS (1952).

The *second generation* machines were initially marked by either magnetic drum or magnetic core storage and, later, by the use of the transistor in place of vacuum tubes.

Under the joint sponsorship of the U.S. Air Force and office of Naval Research, WHIRLWIND I was designed and developed between 1947 and 1951 at the Massachusetts Institute of Technology. It used a cathode ray tube store, but this was replaced in 1952 by the first successful use of a magnetic core memory. The attributes of magnetic core are compactness, reliability and speed of access. However, it took another six years before this type of store was widely used by the industry. The IBM 605 provides an example of an early magnetic drum

6. "The Origins of Digital Computers - Selected Papers" - see Bibliography.

machine which sold far in excess of the original sales estimate (1000 as opposed to 50).

Although the transistor was invented in 1948, several years of development and trial passed before it made any real impact upon the computer industry. The break-through came in 1954 when the Philco Corporation developed a transistor which was to lead to high-speed machines as well as ones with increased capacity. Within four years vacuum tubes were obsolete.

The NCR 304, a joint effort between its designers, the National Cash Register, and its builders, General Electric, was the first all-transistorized computer. However, few were sold due to its relatively slow performance and its limited capacity.

The distinction between second and third generation computers has been a hotly debated point. Those manufacturers who based their new product lines on integrated circuits claimed this to be the dividing line. Whereas those who had not incorporated integrated circuits, preferred to claim that the performance of the system (multi-programming, time-sharing, etc.) characterized the *third generation*. For this reason, we have included a software column in Fig. A1.1. Most of today's computers are classed as third generation machines both in hardware and software.

What of the fourth generation? It seems likely that the new technology which exists today could herald the fourth generation. From the discipline of electronics, computer designers have been given 'large scale integration' (LSI), i.e. many components in a very small space, and semi-conductor memories. This could mean changes in central processor structure, main memory, backing stores and even in computer systems themselves.

What does it all mean? Through LSI techniques, it is now possible to build over 20,000 components onto a small piece or chip of silicon about ¼" square. This technique has enabled the public at large to realize the benefits of pocket calculators and digital watches. With mass production of these so-called micro-processor chips, their cost can fall dramatically as witnessed by the sudden reduction (as well as improved performance) of the pocket calculator over the past few years.

With a similar revolution taking place in the semi-conductor field, via metal oxide silicon (MOS) and bipolar technology, very cheap and potentially large main memories can be attached to the micro-processor to construct micro-computers[7] at a fraction of the cost and size of current mini-computers. To put these latest computers into perspective, let us compare a Fairchild product, the F8, which allows I/O access to the micro-computer via teletype terminals, with one of the earliest computers, the ENIAC.

ENIAC occupied 3000 cubic feet; the F8 takes up 0.011 cubic feet (i.e. 300,000 times smaller). The F8 consumes 56,000 times *less* power;

has a larger main memory; is 10,000 times *more* reliable than ENIAC; weighs 1lb whereas ENIAC weighed 30 tons. Thus, today, as a result of the new technology, there are machines comparable to the early ones but which are smaller, more reliable, potentially more powerful and less costly.

Even more advances are yet forecast by certain experts. It is commonly accepted that by 1980, one million components will be built onto a small silicon chip, and, in the not too distant future 10 million. Moreover, advances in another area of computer technology (charge coupled devices — CDC — and magnetic bubble memory — MBM), according to some experts, seem capable of replacing our disk units for a fraction of their cost and an increase in capacity. This could well facilitate the present day desire to move away from centralized systems to some form of distributed processing.

COMPUTER MANUFACTURERS

UNIVAC

The departure of Eckert and Mauchly from Pennsylvania University in 1947 led to the formation of the Eckert-Mauchly Computer Corporation which, in turn, gave rise, with amalgamations, to the establishment of the Univac Division of Remington Rand. Under contract to the National Bureau of Census, they designed and constructed the first of the UNIVAC line and this was delivered in June 1951. The Universal Automatic Computer was quite an outstanding machine in terms of technological achievement and for five years it had no peer in the area of data processing. In addition to an ability to handle numbers, it had the capacity to handle alphabetic characters, hence its commercial significance.

The successful completion of UNIVAC I marked the end of an era. It brought to a conclusion the dominance of the universities in the development of computer technology and marked the birth of the commercial computer industry.

By 1952, Remington Rand was the undisputed leader in the young field of computers. Its hardware was far ahead of the rest of the manufacturers. But five years later it lost its pre-eminence to IBM. Saul Rosen[8] puts forward two reasons for this. Remington Rand comprised a number of previously independent companies but failed to integrate them into a unified organization and, secondly, its approach to sales was unimaginative and unaggressive. Today, they deal in the medium to large area with such machines as those in their 90 and 1100 series.

7. See below 'Micro-Computers' page 139.
8. See Bibliography.

IBM

IBM entered the computer field by way of electro-mechanical equipment designed to supplement their punched card machines. They were an established firm with an excellent sales organization. This gave them a sound platform on which to base a large scale computer effort. IBM had established a virtual monopoly in the area of business machines. As early as the 1930's they had marketed calculating/punch machines. They had a great number of satisfied customers, many of whom one day would require computer power.

By 1953, when it was clear that computers could be produced with magnetic core memories, IBM decided to capitalize on this new technology. In 1954, it announced its 705 computer and delivered the finished design in 1955.

It made the UNIVAC I obsolete. Remington Rand had also planned a UNIVAC II model incorporating magnetic core, but so many problems arose during the design stage that the first machine was not delivered until 1957. This two-year gap was sufficient for IBM to gain the lion's share of the market and to give them a lead in the large scale computer field which has never been closed and is only now being effectively challenged.

In order to standardize certain features across a range of computers. IBM developed by 1965 their 360 series. The 360's ranged from the very small to the very large and theoretically, programs written to run on the small 360's would also run (though faster) on all larger models, since the smaller models were designed to simulate the larger. This philosophy has made a tremendous impact upon the computer industry and the concept of a range of models has now been adopted by other manufacturers. The 370 series was their next development and it is said to be three or four times as cost-effective as the equivalent 360's.

Today, IBM is the largest computer manufacturer in the world, with sales amounting to 70% of the market, though less than 40% of the U.K. market.

CDC

The birth of Control Data Corporation and its rise to fortune is one of the cinderella stories of the industry. A group of UNIVAC employees broke away and formed Control Data in 1957. As a team they designed, developed and had an order for a machine within three years. Their first, the 1604, was delivered in 1960. This was not as powerful as the equivalent current IBM machine, the 7090, but was much lower priced.

In 1963, they announced the 3600 series which established them as a major organization in the large scale computer market. They made an all-out effort to sell to universities and to gain government contracts.

The company has grown at a considerable rate, with its products covering the whole range from small to large, though with the emphasis on the larger computer, notably the CDC 6400, CDC 6600 and the CDC 7600. The European Centre for Nuclear Research (CERN) was one of the first to order and receive the CDC 7600, whereas Manchester University was the first to do so in England. Recently, CDC has released its CYBER 170 range which, basically, is a development of their 6000 series. The latest machine, called STAR, is one of the world's largest computers and is especially relevant to on-line terminals. Several have already been installed (in America), the first at Lawrence Livermore Laboratories, California.

Honeywell and Burroughs were two other companies to establish themselves and to survive the early period. They both developed from the amalgamation of smaller companies.

Burroughs

Burroughs market medium to large computers, notably their 6700 and 7700. In this country, their machines are used by some of the banks, and have been selected for the Police National Computer Unit for the purpose of bringing together files from Police Criminal Record Offices, Vehicle and Local Authority Indexes.

HIS

Today, Honeywell Information Systems is the second largest computer company in the world. It was formed in 1970 by a merger between Honeywell and GEIS (General Electric Information Systems). There are separate ranges of machines: the medium to large 6000 series, used extensively for time-sharing, and the 60 series.

THE DEVELOPMENT OF THE U.K. INDUSTRY

Following the pioneer work at the universities, two types of firms entered the computer field. These were the established manufacturers of electrical equipment, such as AEI, EMI Electronics, Elliott Bros, English Electric and Ferranti; and the manufacturers of office machinery (e.g., punched-card equipment) notably De La Rue Bull Machines and ICT (International Computers and Tabulators).

By 1960 the manufacture of computers was a substantial British industry. However, there were too many comparatively small firms competing for a rather specialized market. Partnerships between firms from the two categories, electrical and office machinery, sprang up for mutual benefit. These in turn were followed by larger partnerships.

ICT, EMI Electronics and Ferranti linked to form ICT Ltd; and English Electric, Leo Computers and Marconi merged to form the English Electric-Leo-Marconi Company. In 1965, ICT Ltd. finally linked with Plessey and with the English Electric-Leo-Marconi Company to form International Computers Limited (ICL), thus finally establishing a U.K. company large enough to compete with the American giants.

ICL

ICL is now the largest computer company outside the U.S.A. and ranks seventh in the world market, though it holds slightly more of the United Kingdom market than IBM. It has become particularly strong in the public sector, with contracts to government departments, local authorities and nationalized industries. It markets several series of computers; the 1900 series with ICT origins, and System 4, formerly English Electric; its current ICL range is the 2900 series. The 2970 and the 2980 machines are the larger machines in this series and are comparable in performance with the CDC CYBER 170 series and the large IBM 370 machines. The 2980 is four times as powerful as the 2970. Some universities in the U.K. and the European Scientific Research Organization (ESRO) make use of the ICL 2980.

MINI-COMPUTERS

The mini-computer evolved from specialized process control computers and from the aerospace industry of the early 1960's where there was a need for a computer which was small in size and low in weight. The first genuine minis appeared in 1962 and include the Hughes HCH 201 and the Arma Micro Computer but 1965 was the year of the first mass-produced mini, the PDP8, by the Digital Equipment Corporation (DEC). By 1970, there was a marked increase in the number of mini-computer manufacturers.

It is difficult to define a mini since each authority will select its own criteria which, very often, have to include technical considerations. One, almost bizarre definition in 1972 restricted mini-computers to those under 50 lb weight. However, price is one of the more acceptable criteria and today the average price of a mini-computer is about £5000 but this price is for the central processor alone. Buyers still have to purchase peripherals and secondary storage in order to possess a working mini-computer system.

The advantages of minis over the traditional large (mainframe) computers are primarily cheaper processing, smaller size, ruggedness — thus requiring less in the way of environmental control. Today they are used in a variety of applications; within education; in local government; acting as 'front end processors' to a larger mainframe; in transfer of data in time-sharing systems; in industrial and military process control where, being robust and reliable, they become the natural choice over large computers in adverse environments; in word-processing; as well as in commercial and business applications, especially where it is necessary to de-centralize computing power.

Of the above applications, there is one which deserves more comment, namely, the small business system. Mini-computers lie at the heart of these systems to carry out the relatively straightforward functions common to many business and commercial organizations — invoicing, sales analysis, ledger routines, stock control, payroll, job costing, client costing, etc. With the advent of low-cost computer hardware and specialized package programs, it is possible for these business systems to be virtually 'tailor-made' for the professional accountant, solicitor, etc., and to be competently used by secretarial staff with a limited appreciation of computing.

Manufacturers include Computer Technology, NCR, Philips, CII, Hewlett-Packard, Wang, Data General, as well as those already mentioned, i.e. ICL (2903), DEC (PDP8), etc.

MICRO-COMPUTERS

In 1971, Intel produced the first micro-processor on a single chip, the Intel 4004. Since then a great deal has been written about the future impact of these processors upon society and the manufacturing industry as a whole. Predictions vary from unrestrained joy to deep gloom. What is this latest wonder, this micro-processor?

The advent of the micro-processor is due to advances in the field of large-scale-integration (LSI) technology. Although integrated circuits were first produced in the late 1950's, the technology for building them has increased in sophistication with each passing year to the extent that today many thousands of components can be built onto a single chip which contains all the necessary arithmetic and logic functions for a computer processor. These processors are called micro-processor units (MPUs). By themselves, they are not computers since they correspond to the ALU and control units, but when the familiar and additional units (memory, input/output, etc.) are connected they can become micro-computers.

At the same time, tremendous advances made in the area of semi-conductor memories have meant that memory chips can be manufactured which like the MPU chip are very small and very cheap. There are various types of memory chips. Three of the most common are, random access memories (RAMs, into which data can be read or written) i.e. they correspond to the main memory of the conventional computers; read only memories (ROMs) and programmable read only memories (PROMs). The ROM chips are memories containing previously written data which is "burnt" into the chip at manufacturing time, and thus it cannot be altered. These chips, then, can only be used in situations in which it is known that the data need never be altered. Furthermore, when the power supply is turned off, the information or bit patterns in the memory will not be lost (non-volatile storage), unlike some traditional memories, for example, magnetic cores. PROM chips, on the other hand, are memories which *can* have their information altered. These memories are also non-volatile and their advantage over ROMs is that the user can program (and correct if necessary) his own PROM. When an I/O interface device is connected up to the memory chip and the MPU, then one has a micro-computer system. The I/O interface allows an I/O peripheral (often a teletypewriter) to be used.

The importance of these micro-computer systems cannot be overstated. Because of their small size, low cost and high reliability, they are of interest not only to the computer industry but to the industrial community at large. Already, micros are being used in a variety of applications. Apart from the DIY enthusiasts' market, micros are used in the consumer/institutional market for educational toys and games (as well as in T.V. and fruit machines); programmable timing and control in consumer devices such as washing machines, micro wave ovens, refrigerators, and taxi-meters, and in word processing and other office machines; point of sale devices where sales information is processed and then stored on magnetic tape cassettes; security devices; computer peripherals; as well as other areas where miniaturization is vital, such as airborne, space and military applications.

Currently, 4 bit, 8 bit and, more recently, 16 bit processors are available. The 16 bit processors with a reasonable memory size can now be used where previously a small mini-computer would have been required. It will not be long before the 32+ bit processors are commercially available, the 64K RAM chip and a million components built onto a single chip. Where all this will lead the computer industry and, much more important, our society as a whole, it is difficult to predict, in much the same way that a hundred years ago, Alexander Bell could not have predicted the future organization of society as a result of the impact of the telephone upon present-day communications.

2
Programming Languages

Programming languages are divided into two major categories, low-level and high-level. Low-level languages comprise machine languages (illustrated in chapter 5) and assembly-level languages. High-level languages are divided into four classes; scientific, business, specialized and interactive languages. However, there are many hundreds of programming languages and it would be impractical to go into all of them in any detail. The chart in Fig A2.1 attempts to summarize some of the more common (in the sense of popular) languages and shows where and by whom they are used.

The rest of this appendix is devoted to a brief discussion about a few of the more *universal* high-level languages. They are called 'universal' simply because most manufacturers have taken the precaution to supply the necessary language translators which convert these popular languages into the machine code of their own computers. Several languages from each of the scientific, business and interactive groups have been chosen.

FORTRAN — (Formula Translator)

The first available high-level language was FORTRAN, developed in 1956 for use on an IBM 704 computer. Its prime purpose was to solve mathematical and scientific problems which were allowed to be written in a simple English style with the mathematical expressions stated naturally, e.g., $A = B + C - D$.

During the middle 1960's, it became widely used on a number of machines resulting in a variety of 'dialects', the most important being IBM FORTRAN II and IBM FORTRAN IV. By 1962, the American Standards Institute (ASA) set up a working party to produce a specification for the language. Two versions were finally approved in March 1966, ASA FORTRAN (similar to IBM FORTRAN IV) and ASA BASIC FORTRAN (similar to IBM FORTRAN II). Their popularity grew to such an extent that most manufacturers had to insure that their dialect of FORTRAN conformed to these standards.

In August 1966, the ASA changed its name to the United States of

Language Groups	Low-Level	High Level			
	Machine/Assembly Languages	Scientific Languages	Business Languages	Specialized Languages	Interactive Languages
Languages	dependent upon design of machines	ALGOL 60, ALGOL 68, APL, FORTRAN, Pascal, PL/1	COBOL, PL/1	APT, CORAL 66, LISP, RPG, SIMULA, SNOBOL	APL, BASIC, JOSS, Interactive Fortran, RTL/2
Institutions where used	computer centres, bureaux, software houses, industry, commercial companies, universities — all places where systems are developed	universities and research centres	business, commercial organizations	colleges, universities, control plants (industry)	schools, universities, industrial/commercial organizations — all places where real-time and time-sharing applications are in use
Used by	systems programmers, hardware and software manufacturers, as well as some commercial programmers	mathematicians, engineers, chemists, physicists, scientists	data processing and commercial programmers	programmers in specialized applications	programmers in real-time and time-sharing environments

Fig. A2.1

America Standards Institue (USASI) and, this was changed in October 1969 to the American National Standards Institute (ANSI). When people refer to *standard* FORTRAN today, they usually refer to the standards first laid down by ASA in 1966 and which continued unchanged through USASI and ANSI. A new "standard" FORTRAN called FORTRAN 77 has recently been proposed. It contains several additional features which are not a part of FORTRAN IV, e.g. character data types.

ALGOL — (Algorithmic Language)

Like FORTRAN, this language was intended for the solution of numeric and scientific problems, and it differs little in scope from FORTRAN. ALGOL was originally developed in 1958, resulting in ALGOL 58. It was revised in 1960 and the importance of this version (ALGOL 60) lies in the elegance of its structure, something which, historically, will remain long after its demise.

The revised ALGOL 60 report introduced into the computing milieu structural concepts, a precision of language definition, and a certain discipline of programming procedures. These features in FORTRAN had, in contrast, been basically simple.

The most recent, and more powerful, version is ALGOL 68. ALGOL is more popular in Europe than America, where IBM, which is influential in the States, has favoured FORTRAN rather than ALGOL.

Pascal

Pascal (not an acronym, for once, but named after the great Frenchman) is one of those high level languages which the enthusiast claims is a joy to use. It was originally designed by Niklaus Wirth in 1968, belongs to the ALGOL stable and the first operational compiler became available in 1970. One of its more important features is to allow the programmer to structure data in *his* way. Standard Pascal was originally developed and implemented on the CDC 6000 series but has been developed for use on other machines. It is well thought of as a programming language for student teaching and is becoming a highly popular language.

COBOL — (Common Business Oriented Language)

An international business language was inspired by the U.S. Department of Defense in order to handle its many everyday commercial problems. COBOL came out around 1958. It attempts to be a subset of English and is meant to be readable by non-programmers. Its data structures, therefore, were devised to facilitate everyday office file procedures.

Unfortunately, COBOL has not lived up to the original expectations and cannot be fully understood by the uninitiated (office managers), and its propensity towards English has turned it into a verbose language (from the programmer's point of view), yet it remains the most widely used commercial language.

PL/1 — (Programming Language 1)

By the early 1960's, a programmer had a choice of languages. For numeric work there was FORTRAN or ALGOL; for systems programming some assembly language would be preferred; COBOL was used for commercial applications, whilst for more specialized applications such as list processing or string manipulation, there was LISP or SNOBOL. Some installations were beginning to find such a plethora somewhat difficult, not only from an educational aspect but also in the support and maintenance of such a large number of language translators. PL/1 was the intended panacea.

PL/1 was developed in the middle 1960's in an attempt to combine the features of these earlier languages. The intention was to create a language which would be adequate for programming *any* kind of application. This resulted, of course, in the production of a language which is enormous by any standards and one that is not easy to learn in its totality. Furthermore, it was developed by IBM and its use is limited to the equipment of this one manufacturer.

Over the past decade, it has not captured the attention originally anticipated. The current trend in language design is not towards the large language but towards smaller and more elegant ones, e.g., APL. The few features which they possess can be combined by the programmer in such a way as to create, in effect, an individual language for each application.

RPG — (Report Program Generator)

RPG offers an example of a popular commercial language which is also a specialized language. Languages such as FORTRAN and COBOL are general purpose languages, i.e. they are used by people who have many types of programs to write and who wish to use the same language for all their programs. RPG on the other hand can only be used for generating reports, but reports in a broad sense to include the preparation of invoices and cheque payments, as well as "normal" reports.

The language was developed by IBM as a result of their customer requests for an easy and economic mechanism for producing reports and was launched in 1961 for use on the IBM 1401 computer. Today, RPG is run on IBM 360/370 series and the System 3 as well as several other makes such as the ICL 2903 and Univac 9000 series.

When System 3 was introduced by IBM, it was announced that it would use RPG II. This latter version retains all the features of RPG but contains some additional features such as the ability to work with arrays.

APL — (A Programming Language)

APL, designed for time-sharing, is derived from the formal mathematical notation invented in 1962 by Kenneth E. Iverson. The notation, developed by Iverson during graduate courses given at Harvard and later at the IBM Systems Research Institute in New York, is described in his book.[1] The APL system, known as APL/360, was developed by Iverson together with Adin D. Falkoff, Larry M. Breed and staff of the IBM/APL Scientific Centre, and released as an experimental time-sharing service for internal IBM use (at the IBM Watson Research Centre) in the autumn of 1966. It was not until 1968 that APL/360 was first released for public use.

Proponents of APL proclaim it as a consistent, concise and very powerful programming language. Much of its power is vested in the rich set of operators available, enabling easy manipulation of matrices and arrays of highest rank.

APL programs are capable of handling text as well as numerics. It has been used in most fields of programming, but less obvious uses include text editing, system simulation and teaching. The APL user utilizes the system from a terminal device in a **conversational** manner.

BASIC — (Beginners All-Purpose Symbolic Instruction Code)

A language designed primarily for use on time-sharing computer systems. To understand an interactive programming language like BASIC it is not necessary to learn complex programming techniques. It is, in fact, intended for those who have no experience with using computers or writing computer programs. BASIC has few grammatical rules and can be said to be user rather than system orientated. It resembles FORTRAN in many respects, making use of standard mathematical notation, but serves business applications equally well. It can be learnt in a few hours concentrated study and, though simple, it is flexible and reasonably powerful. The language was developed by Professors John Kemeny and Thomas Kurtz (see Bibliography) in the mid-sixties at Dartmouth College in the United States, for use on a time-sharing system, but most of BASIC is equally well suited to a batch-processing environment. Because of its simplicity and bias towards the user, it is a language well suited for use in education.

---

1. "A Programming Language" - K.E. Iverson; Wiley, 1962.

3
Decision Tables

Decision tables have been in existence for a number of years. The era of initial development took place in the late 1950's when General Electric of the United States made the first significant use of such tables. The idea of using a table to lay out or formalize information is not new, e.g. train/airport arrival-departure tables, cricket score boards (tables), are part of everyday life.

Decision tables in computer usage have the same aim of trying to display information clearly and at a glance; but the information is restricted to "what actions to take as a result of some decision". In other words, certain conditions are specified in tabular format as well as the resulting actions.

EXAMPLE 1 : SERVICING A CAR

Let us take a simple example of servicing a car. We might ask "Is petrol low?" "Is oil low?". These two conditions lead to four possible combinations:

> 1) both petrol and oil are low;
> 2) only petrol is low;
> 3) only oil is low;
> 4) neither is low.

Each of the above will result in a different activity:

> 1) get petrol and oil;
> 2) get petrol only;
> 3) get oil only;
> 4) get neither.

In table form, this can be set out as shown in figure A3.1, where each column shows the actions to be taken as the result of a different combination of conditions. A little jargon is now necessary — but it is quite simple and painless. The table is divided into two horizontal and two vertical bands resulting in four distinct areas or quadrants.

CONDITIONS				
1.	IS PETROL LOW	Y	Y	N	N
2.	IS OIL LOW	Y	N	Y	N
ACTIONS				
1.	GET PETROL	X	X		
2.	GET OIL	X		X	
3.	GET NEITHER				X

Fig. A3.1

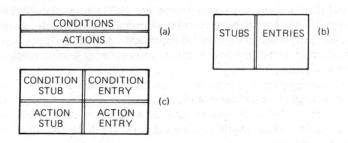

Fig. A3.2

The quadrants are usually separated by double or thick black lines. If the stub (sometimes called statement/logic/parameter) portion completely defines the condition (or action), it is called a *limited entry,* since the entry sections are not required to complete the condition stub or the action stub. Figure A3.1 shows examples of limited entries in both condition and action stub. If the stub portion does not completely express the condition (or action) then it is called an *extended entry.* In these cases, the entries must contain more information than merely YES, NO or X to indicate action.

The final piece of jargon to contend with is the *rule;* this consists of a set of both conditions and resulting actions where one rule corresponds to one vertical column in the entry section. For example, in figure A3.1, rule 2 states "if petrol is low (i.e. Y = YES) and oil is not low (N = NO)," then the action to take is "get petrol only (denoted by an X)."

EXAMPLE 2 : MAIL ORDERING

Let us now take another example and suppose that we have a mail ordering firm sending out literature to various groups of people. These groups are:

group 1 — females between 25 and 60
group 2 — females under 25
group 3 — males under 60
group 4 — males and females 60 and over

If our firm has computerized its mailing system, then a program will exist which will "look at" the sex and age of a given individual and place him/her in one of the groups. Forgetting about decision tables for the moment, let us attempt to construct that part of the program plan which will identify the group an individual will be classed in. Rather than use flowcharts, we shall use the simpler "tree-chart" method. Various charts could be drawn, the one we demonstrate favours finding G4 and G3 more quickly since it "recognizes" an individual in one of these groups more quickly than a G1 or G2 individual.

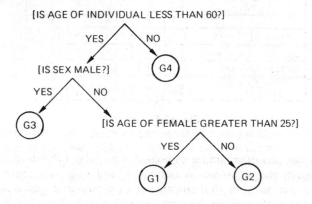

Note that the tree-chart merely describes in a two-dimensional way the necessary program logic (conditions, decisions) to arrive at any one of the four groups. This is all a decision table will show — just the logic — but in a more direct manner. Figure A3.3 shows the decision table and it is useful to point out that the order of the conditions is not import-

CONDITION NUMBER	CONDITIONS	RULE NUMBER				
		1	2	3	4	
1	AGE less than 60	Y	—	Y	N	Limited entries
2	AGE greater than 25	Y	N	—	—	
3	SEX IS MALE	N	N	Y	—	
ACTION NUMBER	ACTION	ACTION NUMBER				Extended entry
		1	2	3	4	
1	CLASSIFY AS GROUP	G1	G2	G3	G4	

Fig. A3.3

ant. Any order could be used whereas with the tree-chart many different charts could be drawn each one arriving at a particular group first.

The dashes (—) used in the columns under the rule heading indicate that the corresponding conditions are irrelevant. Note that the *action* is an extended entry since the complete action to be taken can only be fully stated by looking (extending one's search) into the action entry quadrant.

Had dashes not been used, how many rules would we have ended up with? There is a simple way to find out. If c stands for the number of conditions, then 2^c will be the number of rules. In our case c = 3, thus, $2^3 = 8$ is the correct number of rules. Figure A3.4 shows all eight rules.

CONDITIONS		RULES							
		1	2	3	4	5	6	7	8
1	AGE less than 60	Y	Y	Y	Y	N	N	N	N
2	AGE greater than 25	Y	Y	N	N	Y	N	Y	N
3	SEX IS MALE	Y	N	N	Y	Y	Y	N	N
	CLASSIFY AS GROUP.....	G3	G1	G2	G3	G4	?	G4	?

Fig. A3.4

However, certain rules can be combined, e.g., rules 1 & 4 both lead to a G3 result, therefore one is redundant and both rules may be combined. It can be seen that the answer to condition 2 (age greater than 25) is irrelevant and can be replaced with a dash. The same technique can be applied to rules 5 and 7. Both lead to a G4 indicating that the answer to condition 3 is irrelevant and may be replaced with a dash and the two rules combined (see fig A3.5). It can also happen because of a certain relationship between some conditions that an apparent ambiguity or impossible situation arises. If we look more closely at rules 6 and 8 it is not possible for either of these rules to occur because the answer to conditions 1 and 2 cannot both be NO at the same time. Therefore, by combining rules 1 and 4, 5 and 7 and removing rules 6 and 8 the number of rules can be reduced from eight to four as we had in figure A3.3.

A little more study will reveal that only one answer is really necessary to arrive at a G4, *viz*, a negative reply to condition 1 (AGE *less than* 60). It is sheer redundancy to ask for an answer to condition 2. This can also be seen for rule 2 of figure A3.3, hence the redundancy of condition 1.

It is clear that decision tables do not describe the total program but only that part which involves the logic/decisions/conditions of a certain

CONDITIONS		RULES							
		1	4		R3	5	7		R4
1	AGE less than 60	Y	Y		Y	N	N		N
2	AGE greater than 25	Y	N	becomes	–	Y	Y	becomes	Y
3	SEX IS MALE	Y	Y		Y	Y	N		–
ACTION	CLASSIFY AS GROUP......	G3	G3		G3	G4	G4		G4

Fig. A3.5

section of the program. Since this logic information is captured in tabular form, it is easier to read than an equivalent flowchart or tree chart which in addition to the logic must also show the sequence in which individual decisions are taken in order to arrive at the actions. In this sense decision tables contain *less* information. Consequently, decision tables are not seen as an alternative to flowcharts or tree charts but as a supplement or complement. They are useful to determine whether any combination of conditions have been omitted, this is less easy to achieve with a flowchart.

CONCLUSIONS

Decision tables provide a useful documentary aid between the systems analyst and the programmer. Thus, the programmer responsible for the total plan of the eventual program may include a symbol at a given point in his flowchart indicating that the actual decision table will have to be 'consulted' at that point in order that the conditions may be processed and the resulting action determined. After the 'consultation', the program plan continues in the usual way – figure A3.6 illustrates.

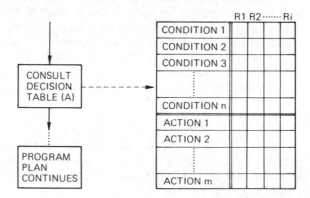

Fig. A3.6

At an early stage in the development of decision tables and high-level languages, it was recognized that the decision table could be converted into program instructions. The first table translators emerged in 1965 but due to their limited ability were little used. Much improved 'second generation' translators became available from 1970 and are now more widely used for many high-level languages such as COBOL, FORTRAN and RPG.

Decision tables have not been examined in great detail since their use implies practical involvement with a computing project. (Readers who wish to pursue this topic are encouraged to refer to the bibliography.) The examples provided here are of a trivial nature and in practice would not warrant the use of a decision table. Clearly, they are of most value when the conditions are numerous as, say, in deciding a premium rating for a life insurance policy. Current translators are capable of accepting not only limited entries (a limitation of the first generation) but also, extended entries; they can produce program instructions equivalent to the best 'hand coded' versions that human programmers achieve; and can also check for completeness, lack of redundancy and ambiguity.

4
BASIC

This appendix is not intended as a comprehensive discussion of BASIC. It is included for those readers who would like to see in a little more detail what is entailed in programming in a high-level language. It provides a few essential definitions and three program examples. Those who wish to pursue the subject further should refer to the Bibliography.

The vocabulary of a programming language is limited to a small number of key words (commands). The format and use of each command is governed by a set of precise rules and a programmer is forced to work within this framework. In the case of BASIC, the syntax is simpler than that of most other programming languages. There are fewer key words and fewer constraints on their use. BASIC is a straightforward language which can be learnt in a very short space of time. It can be used very effectively without the need for developing the programming techniques associated with the efficient use of so many other languages.

Elements of the BASIC language

A statement (program instruction) in BASIC always begins with a line number. The statement has to be completed in one line and its length is limited, typically, to 72 characters (the length of a normal line output at a terminal). The line numbers, unique to each statement, indicate the order of the program and serve as pointers within the program; GO TO 80 literally means jump to the statement beginning with the number 80 and continue executing the program at that point.

Variables are used as 'location names' to identify values which may change during program execution. The values may be numeric or sequences (strings) of characters.

A *numeric variable* (one representing a number) is named with a single alphabetic character, or with a single alphabetic character followed by a single digit:

e.g.   B   M1   Q   F6

LET B = 27 stores 27 in a variable known as B

A *string variable* (one representing a sequence of alphanumeric characters) is named with a two character identifier. The first character is alphabetic and the second is a pound (or dollar) sign:

e.g.   A£   P£   W$

> LET A£ = "COMPUTERS AND COMMONSENSE" stores the string of characters in a variable known as A£. (The maximum number of characters which a string may contain is determined by the machine in use).

BASIC uses certain special symbols for *arithmetical* and *relational* (comparison) operators:

Arithmetical	Meaning	Relational	Meaning
↑	exponentiate (raise to the power) e.g., $X↑3 = x^3$	=	is equal to
		< >	does not equal
		>	greater than
*	multiply	<	less than
/	divide	> =	greater than or equal to
+	add	< =	less than or equal to
—	subtract		

Summary of BASIC Commands

This summary concerns itself only with a subset of the language, consisting of the more straightforward statements which are frequently used in program writing. There are only 13 commands in this subset.

Statement   *Function*

DATA   Directs data to a block of store during the compilation of the program so that the data is accessible (via a READ statement) when the program is executed.

DIM   Declares the size (dimension) of a list or array to indicate the number of storage locations to be associated with the variable name.

END   Indicates the conclusion of the set of instructions and terminates the program in execution.

FOR   Initiates a loop, setting up a counter to control the number of times the loop is to be repeated. It is always associated with a NEXT statement, the pair together controlling the looping procedure.

GO TO — Transfers control to a specified line number, thereby interrupting the numbered sequence.

IF ....
THEN — Transfers control to a specified line number if the condition which is tested is found to be true.

INPUT — Enters data during program execution. At the command INPUT the program prints a question mark and waits for an item of information (or more) to be entered (keyed-in at a teletype terminal).

LET — Assigns a value during program execution.

NEXT — Marks the return point of the loop, incrementing the counter each time the loop is executed until the loop has been completed the number of times specified by the FOR statement.

PRINT — Prints out information.

READ — Assigns values from the data block (created by DATA statements) to the variables listed by the statement.

REM — Inserts remarks for the purpose of documenting the program. This statement is not an instruction which requires any action to be taken, i.e., it is non-executable.

STOP — Terminates the execution of a program at a point other than the END statement.

In addition, BASIC statements exist which enable the programmer to create and read from separate files of data; to access functions (e.g., square roots and logarithms); and carry out matrix operations; and to split up, join together and extract strings of characters.

PROGRAM EXAMPLES

To suggest the flavour of the language, we include three working examples. In an attempt to make the examples easier to follow, only commands from the defined subset have been used. The programs may, therefore, not be written in the most efficient way.

EXAMPLE 1: Program to find the average of three numbers
Program Listing[1]

```
1C REM AVERAGING PROGRAM
2C LET X = 7
3C LET Y = 11
4C LET Z = 6
5C T = X + Y + Z
6C A - T/3
7C PRINT 'AVERAGE IS';A
8C END
```

Execution of Program

```
AVERAGE IS 8
```

Program Analysis

Statement Number	Explanation
10	REM is a non-executable statement which allows a remark to be made in the program so that the listing of the statements is easier to understand.
20-40	Assigns the values 7, 11 and 6 to the variables X, Y and Z respectively
50	Retrieves the values stored in X, Y and Z; adds them together, and stores the result in T
60	Retrieves the value stored in T, divides it by 3, and places the result in A
70	Prints out the characters between the quotation marks followed by the value stored in A
80	Terminates the program

EXAMPLE 2: Program to perform search for book title & to print out the name of the author & the shelf number

In this example we place ten titles, together with authors and shelf numbers, in the store of the computer at the beginning of the program. In the real situation, the complete list of all the library books would be stored as a separate file on a back-up storage device. This would then be accessed when needed.

---

1. Single quotation marks are used in this implementation of BASIC to enclose PRINT messages and strings of characters in DATA statements, instead of double quotes as in most versions.

Program Listing

```
00100 REM         LIBRARY SEARCH PROGRAM
00110 DATA 'BASIC PROGRAMMING','KEMENEY,J·G· AND KURTZ,T·E·','H52:8'
00120 DATA 'COMPUTERS AND COMMONSENSE','HUNT,R· AND SHELLEY,J·'
00130 DATA 'J68:17'
00140 DATA 'COMPUTERIZED SOCIETY','MARTIN,J· AND NORMAN,R·D·'
00150 DATA 'J682:9'
00160 DATA 'DICTIONARY OF COMPUTERS','CHANDOR,A·','J681:3'
00170 DATA 'ELECTRONIC COMPUTERS','HOLLINGDALE,S·H· AND TOOTILL,G·C·'
00180 DATA 'J681:5'
00190 DATA 'FORTRAN IV PRIMER','ORGANICK,E·I·','H52:26'
00200 DATA 'FORTRAN PROGRAMMING COURSE'
00210 DATA 'JAMES,E·B·,O BRIEN,F· AND WHITEHEAD,P','H52:35'
00220 DATA 'ORIGINS OF DIGITAL COMPUTERS','RANDELL,B·(EDIT)'
00230 DATA 'J681:22'
00240 DATA 'PRINCIPLES OF BUSINESS DATA PROCESSING'
00250 DATA 'DOCK,V·T· AND ESSICK,E·','K59:27'
00260 DATA 'UNDERSTANDING DIGITAL COMPUTERS','BENREY,R·M·'
00270 DATA 'J68:47'
00275 DATA 'EMPTY','EMPTY','EMPTY'
00280 REM         SET ARRAYS  B£(TITLE), A£(AUTHOR), N£(SHELF NO)
00290 DIM B£(11), A£(11), N£(11)
00300 I = 1
00310 READ B£(I), A£(I), N£(I)
00320 IF B£(I) = 'EMPTY' THEN 350
00330 I = I + 1
00340 GO TO 310
00350 PRINT 'CONTENTS OF LIBRARY LOADED'
00360 PRINT
00370 REM         PROGRAM READY FOR A REQUEST
00380 PRINT 'BOOK REQUESTED';
00390 INPUT T£
00400 FOR K = 1 TO I
00410 IF B£(K) = T£ THEN 460
00420 NEXT K
00430 PRINT T£; ' NOT IN LIBRARY'
00435 PRINT
00440 GO TO 380
00450 PRINT
00460 PRINT T£; ' BY '; A£(K); ' SHELF NO '; N£(K)
00465 PRINT
00470 GO TO 380
00480 END
```

Execution of Program

```
CONTENTS OF LIBRARY LOADED

BOOK REQUESTED? travels with a donkey
TRAVELS WITH A DONKEY NOT IN LIBRARY

BOOK REQUESTED? computers and common sense
COMPUTERS AND COMMON SENSE NOT IN LIBRARY

BOOK REQUESTED? computers and commonsense
COMPUTERS AND COMMUNSENSE BY HUNT,R· AND SHELLEY,J· SHELF NO J68:17

BOOK REQUESTED? stop
```

Program Analysis

Statement Number	Explanation
100	Remark to document the program
110-275	Assigns information to the data block storing it in the sequence in which it is listed. In this case an

	item of information is enclosed in quotation marks
280	Remark (as statement 100)
290	DIM allocates storage space to the string variables, 11 locations to each, so that the string variables B£, A£, and N£ can be used to store lists of associated information
300	Assigns 1 to I for use as a counter within the program
310	Reads the next set of items from the data block storing it as the I-th elements of the string array variables B£, A£ and N£
320	Compares the contents of the I-th element of B£ (the book title) with the string 'EMPTY', which is the last entry in the list of titles, to see if all have been read. If the comparison is TRUE then jump to the statement which is numbered 350
330	Increments the counter by 1
340	Jumps to statement 310
350	Prints out the message enclosed in quotation marks
360	Prints 'nothing', i.e., leaves a line of output clear for spacing purposes
370	A remark
380	Prints out the message. The semi-colon insures that the next item for printing follows on the same line
390	A request for information which will be stored in the string variable T£. At this point, a question mark is printed and the program stops, waiting for the user to key in some information (in this case the title of the book)
400	Sets up a loop for the purpose of retrieving the list of books so that a comparison can be made with that of the requested title The loop has an initial index value of K = 1 a maximum value of I (the total number of books) an increment of 1
410	Compares the K-th book title stored in the string array variable B£ with the title stored in T£. If they match, the program sequence moves to 460
420	Increments the loop counter K by 1 and tests the result against the maximum value of K, which is I. If K is greater than I when incremented, the program proceeds to 430, otherwise it returns to the statement immediately following the corresponding FOR statement (410)

430	Prints the contents of T£ (the book title) followed by the message in quotes
435	Leaves a line of output blank for spacing purposes
440	Jumps to 380
450	Leaves another line blank
460	Prints in sequence the contents of T£, the message in quotes, the contents of the K-th element of A£, the message in quotes, followed by the contents of the K-th element of N£
465	Another line of output to be left blank
470	Jumps to 380
480	Terminates the program

EXAMPLE 3: Program to convert fahrenheit temperature readings to centigrade for given geographical locations and to display the results in chart form

Program Listing

```
10          REM    TEMPERATURE CHART PROGRAM
20          REM    M$ - MONTHS                    N$ - LOCATION
30          REM    X1 - FAHRENHEIT SUM            X2 - CENTIGRADE SUM
40          REM     T - MONTHLY,TEMPERATURES      A$ - HISTOGRAM OUTPUT
50          REM    A1 - AVERAGE(FAHR)             A2 - AVERAGE(CENT)
60          REM    DIMENSION ARRAYS
70 DIM M$(12), T(12), A$(53)
80          REM    READ MONTHS IN ABBREVIATED FORM
90     FOR I = 1 TO 12
100    READ M$(I)
110    NEXT I
120         REM    INITIALISE TEMPERATURE TOTALS
130 X1 = 0
140 X2 = 0
150         REM    READ NAME OF LOCATION AND THE
160         REM    MONTHLY TEMPERATURES IN FAHRENHEIT
170 READ N$
180    FOR I = 1 TO 12
190    READ T(I)
200         REM    SUM THE TEMPERATURES AND CONVERT
210         REM    MONTHLY FIGURES INTO DEGREES CENTIGRADE
220    X1 = X1 + T(I)
230    T(I) = (T(I)-32) * 5/9
240    X2 = X2 + T(I)
250    NEXT I
260         REM    COMPUTE AVERAGE TEMPERATURE IN
270         REM    FAHRENHEIT AND CENTIGRADE USING
280         REM    THE INT FUNCTION TO ROUND OFF THE AVERAGE
290 A1 = INT(X1/12 + 0.5)
300 A2 = INT(X2/12 + 0.5)
310         REM    PRINT HEADINGS
320 PRINT "STATION: ";N$;TAB(25);"AV. TEMP: ";A2;"CENTIGRADE(";A1"F.)"
330 PRINT "-------";TAB(25);"---------"
340 PRINT
350 PRINT TAB(20);"DEGREES CENTIGRADE"
360 PRINT
370 PRINT " -10         0         10        20        30        40"
380 PRINT " ........................................................"
385 PRINT "    .                                                   ."
```

```
390          REM   TAKE EACH MONTHLY TEMPERATURE,
400          REM   SET THE CORRECT NUMBER OF
410          REM   ASTERISKS IN THE ARRAY A$, AND
420          REM   PRINT THEM OUT IN ROWS TO FORM A CHART
430     FOR I = 1 TO 12
440     C = T(I) + 11
450     PRINT M$(I);TAB(2);".";
460       FOR J = 1 TO 52
470       IF J = 52 THEN 560
480       IF J = 51 THEN 540
490       IF J > C THEN 520
500       A$(J) = "*"
510       GO TO 550
520       A$(J) = " "
530       GO TO 550
540       A$(J) = "."
550       PRINT A$(J);
555       GO TO 580
560       A$(J) = M$(I)
570       PRINT A$(J)
580       NEXT J
590     NEXT I
600 PRINT " ................................................."
610 PRINT " -10         0        10        20        30        40"
620 PRINT
630 PRINT
640 NODATA 9999
650          REM   RETURN FOR A FRESH SET OF DATA
660 GO TO 130
670 DATA J, F, M, A, M, J, J, A, S, O, N, D
680 DATA "TORONTO"
690 DATA 22, 21, 30, 42, 54, 64, 69, 67, 60, 49, 37, 27
700 DATA "LONDON"
710 DATA 39, 40, 42, 47, 53, 59, 63, 62, 57, 50, 44, 40
720 DATA "SYDNEY"
730 DATA 72, 71, 69, 65, 59, 55, 53, 55, 59, 64, 67, 70
9999 END
READY.
```

Execution of Program

```
STATION: TORONTO          AV. TEMP:  7 CENTIGRADE( 45 F.)
-------                   --------


                    DEGREES CENTIGRADE

 -10        0        10        20        30        40
 .................................................
 .                                               .
J .*****                                          .J
F .****                                           .F
M .********                                       .M
A .****************                               .A
M .**********************                         .M
J .*****************************                  .J
J .********************************               .J
A .******************************                 .A
S .**************************                     .S
O .********************                           .O
N .*************                                  .N
D .********                                       .D
 .                                               .
 .................................................
 -10        0        10        20        30        40
```

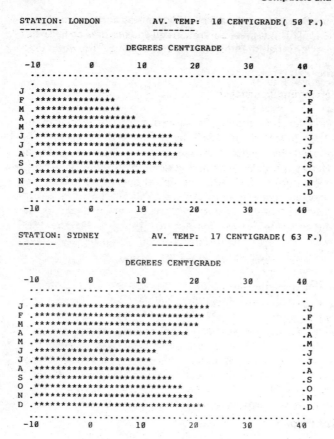

```
STATION: LONDON              AV. TEMP:  10 CENTIGRADE( 50 F.)
-------                       --------

                   DEGREES CENTIGRADE

    -10         0        10        20        30        40
    ...............................................
    .                                              .
  J .**************                                .J
  F .***************                               .F
  M .****************                              .M
  A .*******************                           .A
  M .*********************                         .M
  J .***************************                   .J
  J .*****************************                 .J
  A .****************************                  .A
  S .************************                      .S
  O .*********************                         .O
  N .****************                              .N
  D .**************                                .D

    ...............................................
    -10         0        10        20        30        40


STATION: SYDNEY             AV. TEMP:  17 CENTIGRADE( 63 F.)
-------                      --------

                   DEGREES CENTIGRADE

    -10         0        10        20        30        40
    ...............................................
    .                                              .
  J .*********************************             .J
  F .********************************              .F
  M .*******************************               .M
  A .***************************                   .A
  M .*************************                      .M
  J .**********************                         .J
  J .********************                           .J
  A .***********************                        .A
  S .************************                       .S
  O .***************************                    .O
  N .*****************************                  .N
  D .********************************               .D

    ...............................................
    -10         0        10        20        30        40
```

Glossary

accumulator — part of the ALU consisting of a special register and associated circuitry to perform arithmetic and to store the result.

algorithm — a sequence of statements or rules defining the solution of a problem.

assembler — part of the system software which converts a program written in mnemonics (assembly language) into the machine code which the computer can recognize.

binary digits — bits — the digits 1 and 0 (zero) used in the binary number system.

compiler — a complex program which converts a program written in a high-level language into the machine language which a computer can recognize.

conversational language — a terminal-orientated programming language which allows the user of the terminal to 'converse' with the computer's software (i.e., the language translator and operating system) whilst developing and/or executing a program.

critical path analysis — a technique used in commerce and industry to plan, to control and to schedule major projects.

flowchart — a graphic representation of the step-by-step solution to a problem.

hardware — a term used to refer to the physical units which comprise a computer system; contrasted with software.

hexadecimal — the number system with a base of '16', using the single characters A, B, C, D, E, and F as digits to represent the numbers 10, 11, 12, 13, 14, and 15 respectively.

information retrieval — recovering information from stored data.

integrated circuits — circuits used in third-generation computers in which the components are chemically formed upon a single piece of semi-conductor material.

interface — used generally within computing to refer to a communication link between two otherwise distinct bodies, e.g., the I/O devices act as an interface between the internal world of the CPU and the external world of man.

linear programming — a mathematical technique (not necessarily for computer programming) which produces an optimum value (or ratio of values) for a given situation involving many variables and, for which, no one solution alone is possible.

list processing — concerned with the methods by which lists are processed (ordered and manipulated within central memory) according to certain relationships between the items in the list(s).

location — an area of computer store identifiable by its own address in which a unit of information can be placed.

magnetic core — a small ring of ferro-magnetic matter which can be polarized in one of two states by passing an electric current through wires wrapped around the core.

matrix — used within mathematics to refer to a collection of items arranged in rows and columns, such that to obtain an item both the row number and the column number have to be identified. The frame for noughts and crosses is a square matrix of three rows by three columns.

microfiche — (*fiche* from the French meaning 'card') — a rectangle of film on which a number of frames are recorded in rows. The two standard fiche-sizes, 4 x 6 inches (105 x 148 mm) and 3 x 5 ins (75 x 125 mm approx.) record 60 and 30 frames respectively.

microsecond — one-millionth of a second.

millisecond — one-thousandth of a second.

nanosecond — one thousand-millionth of a second.

octal — the number system with a base of '8', using only the digits 0, 1, 2, 3, 4, 5, 6 and 7.

off-line spooling — the process of transferring information to or from a secondary storage device under the direction of a satellite computer, thus allowing the main CPU to perform other tasks.

operating system — a major part of the system software which essentially supervises the running of users' programs.

packages — a program (or suite of programs) written for general use in a specified application.

peripheral devices — the input, output and storage devices normally operated under computer control.

primary storage — the main store (or memory) of the CPU; also known as main or central memory and immediate access store.

program — a set of instructions which a computer can recognize and which has been ordered in a logical sequence to complete a particular task.

secondary storage — an area of storage separate from the main memory of a computer; synonymous with backing/auxiliary storage.

semi-conductors — used to form small, compact circuitry which can also be used to form memory.

simulation — the representation of a real situation in a computer by means of a 'model' (expressed in mathematical terms) so that different conditions can be tested.

software — a collection of programs written to bring the hardware of a computer system into operation and to best advantage.

string — a sequence of one or more characters.

subset — part of a total set.

transistor — small, light, very fast switching device (also used as an amplifier) within the electronics of second-generation computers.

List of Acronyms

ALGOL	—	*Algorithmic Language*
ALU	—	arithmetic/logic unit
APL	—	*A Programming Language*
APT	—	*Automatically Programmed Tools* — a language for numerically controlled machine tools
BASIC	—	*Beginners All-Purpose Symbolic Instruction Code*
CDC	—	Control Data Corporation
CII	—	Compagnie Internationale pour l'Informatique
CIM	—	*Computer Input Microfilm*
COBOL	—	*Common Business Oriented Language*
COM	—	computer output (sometimes originated) microfilm
CORAL	—	*Class Oriented Ring Associated Language* — for handling certain ring types of lists
CPU	—	central processing unit
CRT	—	cathode ray tube
DEC	—	Digital Equipment Corporation
EDSAC	—	*Electronic Delay Storage Automatic Calculator*
EDVAC	—	*Electronic Discrete Variable Automatic Computer*
ENIAC	—	*Electronic Numerical Integrator And Calculator*
ESRO	—	European Scientific Research Organization
FORTRAN	—	*Formula Translator* language
GEIS	—	General Electric Information Systems
HIS	—	Honeywell Information Systems
IAS	—	Institute for Advanced Study (New Jersey)
IBM	—	International Business Machines
ICL	—	International Computers Limited
ICT	—	International Computers & Tabulators Ltd (amalgamated with other companies to form ICL)
JOSS	—	*Johnniac Open Shop System* — one of the first on-line systems for numerical computation
K	—	kilo, but in computing terminology, the symbol for 1024 (2^{10})
LARC	—	*Livermore Atomic Research Computer*
LEO	—	*Lyons Electronic Office*
LISP	—	language for *List Processing*
LSI	—	large scale integration
MICR	—	magnetic ink character recognition
NCR	—	National Cash Register
OCR	—	optical character recognition
PL/1	—	*Programming Language 1*
RPG	—	*Report Program Generator*
RTL	—	*Real Time Language*

SEAC   — *Standards Eastern Automatic Computer*
SIMULA   — *Simu*lation *Language* — extension of ALGOL for simulation
             problems
SNOBOL   — *String Oriented Symbolic Language*
UNIVAC   — *Universal Automatic Computer*
VDU   — visual display unit

Bibliography

1. **Historical**

    "The Origins of Digital Computers - Selected Papers" - edited by B. Randell; Springer-Verlag, 1973.

    "Electronic Computers; A Historical Survey" - by S. Rosen; Computing Surveys (ACM) March 1969, Vol. 1, No. 1, pp 7-36.

2. **Programming**

    "A Guide to FORTRAN Programming" - by D.D. McCracken; Wiley, 1972 (2nd edition).

    "BASIC Programming" - by J.H. Kemeny and T.E. Kurtz; Wiley, 1971.

    "Principles of Programming - An Introduction with Fortran" - by E.B. James; Pitman, 1978.

    "COBOL for Beginners" - by C. and S. Danziger; Holmes McDougall, 1973

3. **Machine Construction**

    "Thinking Machines" - by Irving Adler; Dennis Dobson, 1961.

    "Processor Architecture" - by S. Lavington; N.C.C. Publications, 1976.

    "Minicomputers" - by P. Sanderson; Newnes-Butterworth, 1976.

    "Simple Computer and Control Logic" - by Schools Council Project Technology; Heinemann Education Books/Schools Council, 1974.

    "Microprocessors - Technology, Architecture and Applications" - by Daniel R. McGlynn; Wiley, 1976.

4. **Operating/Computer Systems**

    "Introduction to Operating Systems" - by A.J.T. Colin; Macdonald/American Elsevier Computer Monographs, 1972.

    "An Introduction to On-Line Systems" - by J.A.T. Pritchard; N.C.C. Publications, 1973.

"The Architecture of Small Computer Systems" - by A.G. Lippiatt; Prentice-Hall, 1978.

"Fundamentals of Data Communications" - by Jerry Fitzgerald and Tom S. Eason; Wiley, 1978.

5. **Data Processing**

"Principles of Business Data Processing" - by V.T. Dock and E. Essick; SRA, 1974.

"Using Computers" - by B. Meek; Wiley, 1977.

"Business Data Systems" - by H. D. Clifton; Prentice-Hall, 1978.

"Introduction to Computers in Business" - by Elias M. Awad; Prentice-Hall, 1977.

"Computer Data Processing" - by Gordon B. Davis; McGraw-Hill Book Company, 1973 (2nd edition).

"Decision Tables" by Michael Montelboro; SRA, 1974.

6. **Applications and Society**

"Computers and Their Uses" - by W.H. Desmonde; Prentice-Hall, 1971.

"Computers and Society" - by S. Rothman and C. Mosman; SRA, 1976 (2nd edition).

Index

accumulator, 26, 27, 66, 70
Aiken, Howard.A., 129
ALGOL, 143
algorithm, 52, 70
ALU, 13, 19
APL, 145
applications, 86f
   business, 87f
   communications, 95f
   industrial, 91f
   local authorities & public
   utilities, 97f
   meteorology, 94
   scientific, 86f
   space technology, 94
Aquinas, Thomas, 8
assembly codes, 61f
   assembler, 62, 76
audio response unit, 44
automation, 122

Babbage, Charles, 3, 128
   Analytical Engine, 3f
   Difference Engine, 3
backing stores, 44f
   direct access, 44
   serial access, 44
bar codes, 39
BASIC, 145, 154f
batch processing, 76f
   off-line spooling, 77
binary, 5,
   arithmetic, 17f
   bit, 5
   counting, 17f
Burroughs, 137

CDC, 136f
   CDC 1604, 136
      6000 series, 7, 137
      CYBER, 76, 137

STAR, 137
CERN, 86,
character set, 15f, 33f
   MICR fonts, 35
CIM, 43
COBOL, 143
coding, 59
   forms, 32
COM, 43
compiler, 62, 65, 71
computer, analogue, 12
computer arithmetic, 19f
computer, characteristics of, 7f
computer, digital, 10, 12
computer languages, 60f
computer word, 15, 17
Comrie, Dr. L.J., 129
console, 74f, 117
control unit, 3f, 26f
CPU, 4, 6, 9, 12f, 50, 79f
   speeds of, 75f
CRT, 41, 133

data base, 90
data processing, 102f
   files, 104f
   records, 104f
DEC, 139
decision tables, 146f
distributed processing, 84f
DP Manager, 117

EDSAC, 131f
EDVAC, 131
ENIAC, 130

file librarian, 117
floppy disk, 47f
flowchart, 52f
   symbols, 53
FORTRAN, 62, 141f

graphical output, 40f
  engineering design, 93f

hardware, 29
HARVARD MK I, 129
high-level languages, 61, 141f
Hollerith, Herman, 32, 129
Honeywell (HIS), 137

IAS, 133
IBM, 129, 136
  IBM 605, 133
       705, 136
       1401/7094/1460, 77
       360 and 370 series, 136
ICL, 138
  ICL 1900 series, 138
       2900 series, 138
ICT Ltd., 137
Imperial College, 77
informatics, 2
information retrieval, 90
input, media & devices, 6, 30f
instruction, 25f
  high-level, 64,
  jump (logical), 68f
  machine, 61, 66
integrated circuits, 15, 133
Intel, 139

key-to-cassette 49
key-to-disk, 49
key-to-tape, 49

von Leibnitz, G.W. 128
LEO, 102
line printer, 40, 75
  electrostatic, 40
location address, 24, 61, 65
logic gates, 22
  AND, 22f
  NOT, 22f
  OR, 22f
LSI, 134

machine codes, 61
machine intelligence, 125
magnetic core memory, 15, 133
magnetic disk, 46f
  disk pack, 46
  fixed-head, 47
  moving-head, 47
magnetic tape, 44f
  tape drive, 45
  speeds, 45, 76

Manchester Mk I, 61, 132
mark & character recognition, 35
mark sense reading, 35f
memory, 8, 24f
  location address, 24, 61, 65
  magnetic core, 133
MICR, 31, 35f
  fonts, 36
micro-computers, 134f, 139f
  micro-processors, 134, 139
microfiche, 43
microsecond, 7
millisecond, 7
mini-computers, 138f
multi-programming, 79f
  memory partitions, 80

nanosecond, 7
Napier, John, 128
NCR 304, 134
networks, computer, 83f
von Neumann, John, 131
number systems, 17f
  binary, 17f
  hexadecimal, 22
  octal, 22

OCR, 31, 37
Operating systems, 65, 78f
  supervisor, 80
  system control commands, 78
  transfer monitor, 80
operation code, 26, 61
operations manager, 117
operators (computer),
output, media & devices, 6, 39f

packages, 73, 116
paper tape, 34f
  reader, 34
Pascal, Blaise, 128
Pascal language, 143
peripheral devices, 30
Philco Corporation, 134
picosecond, 7
PL/1, 144
point-of-sale terminal, 39
privacy, 123
programmers, 116
  applications, 116
  systems, 116
programming languages, 60f, 141f
  high level, 61, 141f
  low level, 62, 141
programming manager, 116

punched card, 32f
    punched card reader, 33
    punch machine, 32

random (direct) access, 44, 107
real-time, 82f
registers, 27
Remington-Rand, 135
RPG, 144

satellite computer, 77
SEAC, 74, 133
security, 123f
semi-conductor, 15, 133
sequential (serial) access, 44, 107
Shannon, Claude, 128
software, 29
storage, 8, 24f
    primary, 29
    secondary, 8, 29
systems analysis, 108f

analyst, 108f
feasibility study, 113

tabulating system, 129
    verification, 33
teletypewriter terminal, 38f
time-sharing, 81f
    time slice, quantam, 81
transistors, 15, 133
Turing, Alan, 128

UNIVAC, 102, 135f
    UNIVAC I & II, 135f

vacuum tubes, 133
VDU, 41f
    graphics VDU, 42
voice recognition, 30

WHIRLWIND I, 133
word processing, 87

**Some other new books from
Prentice-Hall International
66 Wood Lane End
Hemel Hempstead, Herts, England**

BUSINESS DATA SYSTEMS
A practical guide to systems analysis and data processing
H. D. CLIFTON
(Wolverhampton Polytechnic)

This comprehensive, practical text on systems analysis and data processing will provide a broad grounding for students in computer science, business studies and accountancy. It is suitable for courses at colleges, polytechnics and universities, and is geared towards professional examinations.

Management information, rather than technicalities, is emphasised throughout. Exercises and solutions are provided at the end of each chapter, and over 100 diagrams, charts and tables help clarify the text.

Contents: Business and Management Information. Computers in Business. Data Capture and Computer Input. Computer Files and Databases. Computer Output. Programming and Software. Systems Investigation. Design of DP Systems. Systems Implantation. Case Study — Sales. Order Control and Accounting. Glossary of Terminology: Explanation of Terms, Further Reading.

352 pages   Paper
13-093963-3

THE ARCHITECTURE OF
SMALL COMPUTER SYSTEMS

ARTHUR G LIPPIATT
(The Hatfield Polytechnic)

Computer architecture is an important area in computing that is of equal interest to computer scientists and electrical engineers. It is the common ground that both software and hardware specialists need to understand. *The Architecture of Small Computer Systems* provides both groups with a readable and straightforward introduction to the basic structure of small computers. *The Architecture of Small Computer Systems* has been fully tested on student courses, and the principles set out in the text are related to some of the most popular commercial computer systems. Technical terms are defined at their first appearance in the book to ensure a full understanding of the topics discussed, and exercises are included at the end of the book. Over one hundred line-drawings and diagrams are provided.

Contents: Introduction to a Computer System. The instruction Set of the Central Processor. The Coding of Information in Computer Systems. Addressing the Memory. Data Transfers within the Computer System. Interrupts and Direct Memory Access. Computer Arithmetic. APPENDIX: Surveys of: NOVA Minicomputer System. PDP 11 Minicomputer System. M 6800 Microprocessor System.

192 Pages
13-044768-4 cloth
13-044750-1 paper

THE WIRED SOCIETY
JAMES MARTIN

James Martin's many highly successful books have won him the reputation of being a leading authority on the latest developments in the fields of computing and telecommunications.

The Wired Society is his vivid prediction of how the world will be changed and shaped by the many uses of telecommunications and its related products. James Martin believes that 'Communications media will soon become essential to society's infrastructure, essential to the way society is governed — the cornerstone of the culture of our time'. He describes a technical revolution where such words as telebanking, telemedicine, teleshopping, telemail will be taken as much for granted as telephone and television today. He prefaces his discussions with historical as well as contemporary references, and provides real and realistic examples to illustrate the society he depicts.

Contents: Technology and the Environment. New Highways. Medical Facilities. Widely Differing Requirements. New Uses of Television. News. Public Response Systems. Spiderwebs. Invisible Money. Instant Mail. Information Deluge. Radio Devices. The Satellite Age. Home. Telephones with Pictures. A substitute for Gasoline. Industry. A 3½-day Week. Education. 1984. The Human Goldfish. Wired World. Who Pays?

240 pages
13-961441-9 cloth

USING OPERATIONAL RESEARCH
A practical introduction to quantitative
methods in management

RICHARD TAFFLER
(City University Business School

Using Operational Research covers the major types of managerial problems soluble by OR methods. It starts with three chapters on financial mathematics — Introduction to Investment Appraisal, Discounted Cash Flow, and Investment Appraisal Techniques — which are of particular relevance to accountancy students. In later chapters it introduces the use of simple computer packages in Operational Research. The book assumes knowledge of only elementary mathematics, and can be used as a self-instruction book or as a course text. It is suitable for managers and future managers as an introduction to Operational Research for business decision-making.

Contents: The Operational Research Approach. Introduction to Investment Appraisal. Discounted Cash Flow. Investment Appraisal Techniques: Some Alternative Approaches. Replacement Strategies. Inventory Control. Critical Path Analysis. Linear Programming. Transportation Problems.

Publication: May 1979
Paperback
13-939835-X